Lifted Up, My Whole Hearted Testimony

By Rachel Rebecca Baxter

"Worship God, for the testimony of Jesus is the spirit of prophecy."

Revelation 19:10 KJV

Lifted Up, My Whole Hearted Testimony—2nd Edition

Scriptures not marked are taken from the NEW INTERNATIONAL VERSION (NIV): Scripture taken from THE HOLY BIBLE, NEW INTERNATIONAL VERSION ®. Copyright© 1973, 1978, 1984, 2011 by Biblica, Inc.™. Used by permission of Zondervan

Scriptures marked KJV are taken from the KING JAMES VERSION (KJV): KING JAMES VERSION, public domain.

Trade Paperback ISBN 978-1-7340508-0-6

Published and printed in the United States by Valor Community Publishing 2019

ACKNOWLEDGEMENTS

I am thankful to my Father, God the creator, and my savior Jesus for redeeming my life. I am thankful for the gift of Holy Spirit living in me – my constant companion and connection to the eternal life I was made for. The Lord was with me in writing each and every page of this book.

I pray a blessing over my husband, Garrick, for his unending patience with me. For 15+ years, he has been the one person on this earth *lifting me up,* encouraging me to be who I was created to be. He has walked this Holy Spirit-filled journey with me the last few years with an open heart to the move of God taking place in our lives. We have faced the attack of the enemy on our marriage and come out with hands firmly clasped together and our eyes locked on Jesus, as we endeavor to raise our own four kids and any other children the Lord calls into our life, according to the purposes of God.

My life is filled to overflowing in no small part due to the friends God has brought into my life. Heidi, Krista, Kari, Tonya and many others have consistently spoken truth into me, even when I didn't want to hear it! Each of you carries the treasures of heaven in your hearts as wives, mothers, and daughters. You have taught me much about living from the perspective of the Kingdom of God. You have caused me to be bold in coming out of the ways of this broken world. The Lord has used you to strengthen me when I was weak from the battle. It is your love that *lifted me* time and time again. I thank God for our friendship in this season.

I am grateful for the incredible blessing of the One Whole Heart Ministry and Healing Community in my life. From the revelation of Papa's heart, Pastor Chuck gave the gift of a lifetime to me, as he has freely given to multitudes one heart at a time. This gift changed everything for me. I can now say that I am a new creation! The old has gone and the new has come!

Lifted Up

Lastly, bless God for the work that He is doing to bring His Kingdom to this earth at this time. I am thankful to have a role to play in bringing the reality of God's plan for His children forward as He speaks identity and destiny into every child that He calls.

> *"So Christ himself gave the apostles, the prophets, the evange-*
> *lists, the pastors and teachers, [12] to equip his people for works of*
> *service, so that the body of Christ may be built up [13] until we all*
> *reach unity in the faith and in the knowledge of the Son of*
> *God and become mature, attaining to the whole measure of the*
> *fullness of Christ."* Ephesians 4:11-13

My Whole Hearted Testimony

CONTENTS

INTRODUCTION

On **June 23rd, 2015** I dreamt that I was reading my Bible, but instead of the first Book of the Bible being Genesis, it was the Book of Revelation. In the dream, I also looked at the Bible on my iPad, and on my phone and all three showed that Revelation was the beginning and not the end.

> *"In the mouth of two or three witnesses shall every word be es-tablished."*   *2 Corinthians 13:1b KJV*

Have you ever wondered why God gives us dreams? Or maybe you have questioned whether your dreams are really from God, or just from the rich meal you had before bedtime. Or maybe you've had dreams that you know are from the enemy, Satan.

Why would God give me a dream that showed Revelation as the first book of the Bible and not the last? Well, I asked Him, and this is what I heard: "Rachel, this is the time you've been chosen to live. You are living in the time of the Revelation of Jesus Christ, Yeshua HaMashiach."

Some of you reading this book may be thinking to yourself right now, "How could this author claim to hear from God for herself? Surely that is blasphemy. She couldn't possibly hear from God directly and then write down what He said."

Well, I will tell you the truth. Six years ago, I would have agreed with you completely. I didn't believe that God would talk to someone as reg-ular as me. I knew that God did speak to special people—at least He used to in "Bible Times", as I was taught from the time I was a very little girl going to Sunday School in a small town in northwest Iowa. I knew all the good stories from the Bible, like the one where God spoke to Abram in his old age to tell him that his wife Sarai would conceive, or when He spoke to Moses up on the mountain as He gave him the Ten Command-ments.

But I didn't know that God could or would choose to speak to someone like me, either through His word, dreams, through visions or that still small voice. There is nothing remarkable about me, apart from God and His work in my life. I'm probably a lot like you. I know what it is to be hurt and to hurt others. I know what it feels like to work so hard to try to somehow 'earn' love from others and even from God, only to feel like I've failed. I know what emptiness, loneliness, and deep depression feels like.

In my college years, after I'd fallen away from my childlike faith in Jesus, it was the thought that the Creator of the Universe, or "higher power", spoke to someone alive today that got me in pretty big trouble spiritually. I came across a series of books called "Conversations with God" where the author claimed that God was speaking to him, and that he was told to write down all that God said to share with the world. Unfortunately, many things this author wrote about did not line up at all with the Scripture, the inerrant Word of God found in the Bible. It turns out this kind of thinking was really "new age" thinking from man (inspired by the enemy himself, the father of lies) and not from God.

I can tell you without a shadow of personal doubt, that God, also called YHWH (The one and only true God, the Father of Abraham, Isaac, and Jacob) does speak to people today. His heart is that every one of His children would hear His voice, choose to listen, and then FOLLOW Him where He leads. Jesus said,

"You are my friends if you do what I command." John 15:14

If you are reading this book, then I believe that the Lord has been stirring something in your heart, or in the hearts of your children or grandchildren. Maybe you've been feeling dissatisfied with the hollow message being spoken in some well-meaning Christian churches today. Maybe you feel an emptiness inside that you just can't seem to fill anymore with shopping, eating, working, drinking, or through consuming large amounts of media.

Maybe you just feel generally exhausted and can't seem to find rest. In my experience, that feeling of longing can only be satisfied one way. I believe that God created us with a missing inward part that can only be filled when we are "plugged in" to Him.

God alone is the missing puzzle piece that was always meant to perfectly complete each of His children.

He has planted a seed in you of His truth and He desires to cause it to grow. My prayer is that my testimony recorded here will be a blessing to you. I pray that what I share, whether from my everyday life, or from my interactions with Holy Spirit and the Spiritual realm, would cause you to challenge the paradigm you currently hold about the one we call "God", and to even cause you to open your mind and heart to who He created you to be in Him.

My prayer for you, dear reader, and for every child of God, is that you would come to know your identity found in Jesus, and the destiny that God planned for you before the foundations of the earth. It is not yet too late to step into who He created you to be! Your life's testimony has not yet been completed, as I hear His voice crying out to you that He has so much more for you to experience in Him!

I wrestled with God for quite some time before agreeing to write this book. When He told me that it was to be my testimony, I thought to myself, why the heck would someone want to read about my life? But then God spoke to my heart and convicted me that all each of us really have is the life we've lived, and if we are so fortunate, the understanding of who He has made us to be. We don't have *much else to give* but who we are and what we've learned.

My hope in sharing my testimony with you is that you would see that God could take someone as lost and broken as me, someone hopelessly dramatically normal, and trade my life in for the life that Jesus bought and paid for on the cross—a supernatural, Holy Spirit-filled life given over to Him and His purposes. You will find that I am far from perfect and have made more than my fair share of mistakes. But you will also find as you read my testimony that God is just as good as He claims to be. It is His love for me (and His love for you) that propels me forward with the deepest desire to come into the fullness of who He created me to be. I pray that what He has done in my life would instill in you the promise of what He can do in your life, as you learn to hear His voice and surrender to His will for you.

I pray that you will take every word that you read here back to the Lord for rebuttal or for confirmation. I'm only human, and am capable of error, though I commit to describing my stories in the truest possible light, sharing with you the experiences of my life—both before and after I met Holy Spirit in October of 2013.

Perhaps in your life, you can point to a moment in time, or an event, that changed everything for you. For me, that moment with the God of the universe has changed everything, sometimes slowly and sometimes like a whirlwind–and I am not exaggerating! My life would not ever be the same after EXPERIENCING God; and the promise He makes to you is that your life will never be the same again once you EXPERIENCE the God of all creation–the God who knew you even before He set the foundations of the earth.

I pray that this book would be a testimony of what Jesus has done in my life, but more importantly, I pray that it would prophetically speak into your life... what God **will do** in your life as you walk out the plans He has for you, which were predestined before time began.

<u>CHAPTER 1: Before the Beginning... I Knew You</u>

"For he chose us in him before the creation of the world to be holy and blameless in his sight. In love [5] he predestined us for adoption to sonship through Jesus Christ, in accordance with his pleasure and will— [6] to the praise of his glorious grace, which he has freely given us in the One he loves...

In him we were also chosen, having been predestined according to the plan of him who works out everything in conformity with the purpose of his will, [12] in order that we, who were the first to put our hope in Christ, might be for the praise of his glory. [13] And you also were included in Christ when you heard the message of truth, the gospel of your salvation. When you believed, you were marked in him with a seal, the promised Holy Spirit, [14] who is a deposit guaranteeing our inheritance until the redemption of those who are God's possession—to the praise of his glory."
Ephesians 1:4-6, 11-14

One of my very earliest memories as a little girl was of flying. I'm not talking about flying on an airplane. I think that I was around three years old at the time of this experience. I can picture even now in my mind's eye being *magically* lifted up high into the air. I can see myself sailing around the ceiling of a small living room area that belonged to my grandparents at the time. I was all alone, except I wasn't. Jesus was with me. (I believe now that Jesus was always with me, just as He is always with you. As a little child, I didn't question His presence in my life be-cause He was there from the beginning.)

I don't remember for sure, but I may have begged him relentlessly to allow me to fly... and He did. He chose to give me the delight of my heart. I do remember trying to tell adults in the years after of this sweet memory, only to be ignored, or worse yet, patted on the head with a terse "Oh that is nice honey" of unbelief.

Eventually, I myself stopped believing that this had happened–until I again met Holy Spirit and came to believe that God and Jesus really love me enough to even answer a little girl's prayer to fly.

Is my experience Biblical? Not in the sense that I can point to a specific example of Jesus answering a silly prayer of a child, but I believe there are numerous Biblical examples of God and Jesus acting supernaturally to answer prayer. Jesus' first recorded miracle was to turn water into wine because of the request of his mother! What my experience with flying showed me was that our God is incredibly good. He is a loving Father who dotes on His children. He knows us intimately well and chooses to pour out His blessings on us. God also knew that on this day, in this book, I would be sharing this experience with you. I pray that this would grow your faith to believe for tiny (or big) miracles in your life.

Just last week I prayed and ask God to give me encouragement. I was feeling weary from the battle of everyday life and responsibilities. He sent me to Matthew 7:7-8 which reads:

> *"Ask and it will be given to you; seek and you will find; knock and the door will be opened to you. [8] For everyone who asks receives; the one who seeks finds; and to the one who knocks, the door will be opened."*

This is the truth. He wants us to come to Him with the little things and the big things in our lives, with the battles and the dreams in our hearts.

Another example of this concept played out in my life involves what I affectionately refer to as my "spirit cat" experience. Not long after I was 'spirit-filled' (which I will go into more detail about in a subsequent chapter), an author and teacher came to town named Blake Healy. I had just finished reading Blake's book called The Veil, which I would highly recommend. As I went to bed that evening, I remember praying a simple prayer that went something like this: "Lord, I'd like to see in the Spirit the way that Blake does. Will you let me see something tonight?"

Lifted Up

Well, late that night I awoke to the sound of purring. I felt the sensation of whiskers moving across my face. I felt a cat jump from the left of my face to the right side of my face, and then down between my calves, and finally off the bed onto the carpet with a "frrr-rump" sound. You know the sound that I mean if you've ever heard a cat jump down from a higher surface to hit the floor. It's like a tiny bit of air being let out of a balloon. As I began to fully wake up, the thought occurred to me that I did not have a cat! What was really remarkable about that was that I *heard* and *felt* the cat but did not *see* the cat. My prayer was that I would see something in the Spirit, but God chose to answer my prayer in a different way. Instead of allowing me to see something with my eyes, in His divine wisdom, He chose to allow me to use two of my other senses instead.

I'd like to point out a key lesson in our growth as believers that can be gleaned from this experience. **God answered my prayer, not according to what I asked** (to see something in the spiritual realm), **but according to what He desired for me** (to hear and feel in the spiritual realm), because He knows me better than I know myself. In that moment, in that answered prayer, the God of the universe did something very intimate. He knew that the one thing in the whole world that I could experience *in the Spirit* without fear in that moment was a cat. You see, from the time I was five years old until I was well into adulthood, I had a cat. However, at that particular time, our family was without a cat.

My first cat's name was Muffy. I first met her when she came up to my best friend at the time, Heather, who was sitting next to me as we played together in the small grove of trees behind our house. Muffy walked up to Heather and literally pooped right there on her shoe! It was an odd thing to do, but thankfully my friend thought it was as funny as I did. Muffy was black and soft, wise and tolerant, and it was love at first sight.

Muffy was adventurous and energetic. She was also motherly. In fact, she was like a mother to me, as strange as that may sound. She was an unshakable presence in my life during my formidable years when my life was full of uncertainty. Muffy was calm and cuddly. She would just sit with me and allow me to pet her and scratch her around her mouth and ears for as long as I was willing to.

My primary love language is touch, so to me, there is nothing that fills me up more than holding a warm animal in my arms. Muffy was forever pregnant with kittens, as she was as fertile as any living creature has ever been. She had at least ten litters of kittens that. We did try to take her to the vet more than once to be *fixed*, but each time the vet would shake his head because she would already be *with child*.

She taught me about life as I got to observe and even participate in the birth of many of those kittens. She also taught me about death, as she would proudly deliver her latest prey (whether bird or mouse) to my feet.

(Back to the Spirit cat story!) Only God could know, having observed me moment-by-moment for 37+ years up to that point, that experiencing a cat that wasn't really physically there but most certainly spiritually there would not scare me. I can honestly say that if God would have allowed me to see (or feel or hear) something else on that night in the spiritual realm, whether angel or demon, at that point in my spiritual journey with Him, I would have been absolutely frightened. But a cat? Nope. I felt peace and joy when I heard the purring and felt the whiskers in the middle of the night. Those were comfortable sensations of a cat lover who was used to cats sleeping in bed with her. God just knew me. He just knew the best and perfect way to answer my prayer. You see, He knew me because He has always known me. The Bible says that He knew us even before the foundation of the world.

King David writes, in Psalms 139:15-16

"My frame was not hidden from you
when I was made in the secret place,
when I was woven together in the depths of the earth.
[16] Your eyes saw my unformed body;

Lifted Up

*all the days ordained for me were written in your book
before one of them came to be."*

Before God created the world that we know today made up of the
earth, the seas, the skies, and the universe of moons, stars, and sun...
He knew me and He knew you.

A couple of years ago, a Christian mentor named Gary asked me this
question, "Why did God create man?" It was a simple question really,
but at the time I struggled to answer it. I thought maybe He created us
because He was bored and wanted a *grand* experiment in free will. Boy,
has that gone poorly for Him! We see how we fall short in every way
imaginable of what He must have intended for us, before sin entered
the world though Eve and Adam through temptation by the serpent,
Satan.

It wasn't until I began to know God's heart, spending time in His word
and with Him in His presence that the answer became obvious: I can
now say that I know *my knower.* He created each one of us for relationship with Him. He did not *need* us. He did not *have* to create us. He
simply chose to create us and everything in this world around us for His
good pleasure.

The God of the universe created you and me as an expression of Himself, each one of us a special and unique reflection of a part of who He
is. We are each like our fingerprints: Not one of us the same as another.
Not one of us any less valuable than another. We know that it is true
that not one of us is the same as another, not even identical twins are
the same beyond their genes, though they may share commonalities.
The truth is that God knew us before we were even in our mother's
womb.

> *"Before I formed you in the womb I knew you,*
> *before you were born I set you apart;*
> *I appointed you as a prophet to the nations."*
> *Jeremiah 1:5*

He not only knew us, but He created us for a purpose. This verse in Jeremiah goes on to say that He created Jeremiah to be a prophet to the nations. You might think that Jeremiah was just special, and that the rest of us are just sheep in a herd, all the same, but that is just not true.

Each child of God was created for a special purpose in Him, with unique gifts and abilities, given just as a unique journey was laid out for each of us through this life on earth. I am the only one who can fulfill my life's purpose in His kingdom, and you are the only one that can fulfill your life's purpose. And He left nothing to chance…

> *"Indeed, the very hairs of your head are all numbered. Don't be afraid; you are worth more than many sparrows. " Luke 12:7*

What is this scripture saying? God doesn't just know you like your spouse knows you, or a close friend. He knows every hair on your head. He knows every thought you've ever had. He knows every mistake you've ever made. He knows every fear and each and every dream you've held in your heart. There is nothing in you beyond His understanding. Let the gravity of that sink in for a moment: The one true God over all chose to make you and me just like we are, and He chose for us to live now, at this time. And it's not random chance but a divine hand that brought you and me to where are today.

God chose for me to be born in 1977 to working-class folks from northwest Iowa. My town of Ireton had and still has about 500 people, give or take one or two depending on births and deaths. There were more churches than bars. The church we attended was St. Paul's Lutheran Church, Missouri Synod, of which my mom was an organist. I was the second child in our family. My sister, Molly, was three years older than me, and four years after me my sister, Greta, was born.

My parents named me Rachel Rebecca. My middle name was handed down from my dad's mom, whose middle name was also Rebecca. I asked my mom recently why they named me like they did, since neither of my sisters were given a Biblical name. She said they just liked the name Rachel and Rebecca seemed to fit well with it. However, I don't believe that is the whole story from God's perspective.

As I've grown in my understanding of God's word and His heart, I've come to believe that God gave my name through my parents for a purpose. Remember: He leaves nothing to chance. Our names matter to God, and we are promised that they are either written in the Book of Life or not. It is of the utmost eternal importance that we find our names there!

> *"The one who is victorious will, like them, be dressed in white. I will never blot out the name of that person from the book of life, but will acknowledge that name before my Father and his angels."*   Revelation 3:5

> *"And I saw the dead, great and small, standing before the throne, and books were opened. Another book was opened, which is the book of life. The dead were judged according to what they had done as recorded in the books."* Revelation 20:12

> *"Anyone whose name was not found written in the book of life was thrown into the lake of fire."*   Revelation 20:15

You can be sure that your name was given for a purpose. Seek God for yourself for understanding. I encourage you to ask Him why you were given your name. Research and find out the meaning of your name, even if you don't think it is *Biblical*. It matters, just like you matter.

Though you may not like your own name, God knew what he was doing when He gave it to you. The Lord recently connected me with a fellow disciple of Jesus who lives in Australia. She sent me this note when she learned my given name:

"It is astonishing that your parents chose for you the names of two of the most important mothers ever. Rebekah (wife of Isaac) gave birth to the twins, Jacob and Esau. Rachel (wife of Jacob) gave birth to Joseph

and Benjamin. First, we have two nations coming from Rebekah's womb - then we have the two houses of Israel represented in Rachel's womb. Joseph fathered Ephraim and Manasseh (of the ten tribes/House of Israel). Benjamin joined his older brother Judah to become the House of Judah. So, within your name, Rachel Rebecca, you are mother to the whole house (twelve tribes) of Israel through Joseph and Benjamin, and Esau too.

For interest (and fun) I looked up the meanings of Rebecca and Rachel. I found Rebecca = 'she knows' and Rachel = 'ewe.' So how about 'she knows the sheep.' I think that is prophetic for you having a knowing of His sheep which is imparted to you by His Spirit. You will firstly recognize them in the crowd (as a mother knows her own child) and you will also know their needs and what to say to them."

That is certainly a glowing description of the birthright that is available through God alone. I have come to recognize the call God put on my life to be a mother not only to my own children but to many children, His children, all over the world. I could only hope to attain the fullness of what He intended for me as I surrender my life to Him. (If what my Australian friend wrote about in terms of the House of Israel and the Twelve Tribes is confusing to you, but you are interested to learn more, check out my next book on the Revelation of Israel.

My point in sharing that with you is simply to speak to your heart to say that who you were created to be, from your name to your journey on this earth, is firmly held in the palm of God's hands. He is waiting to show you who He created you to be.

As a little girl, I had what is commonly referred to (by adults who do not believe in angels) as an "imaginary friend". My angel's name then, and now, is Fred. As a child, I could see Fred at times, and I always felt his presence. I knew that he went wherever I went. Just like Jesus, I did not question his existence, though other people around me disregarded him as a part of my vast imagination.

Lifted Up

Here is the deal: Angels are real and so are demons. They exist, even on this earth. I can't say it any more clearly than that. Many of us don't want to believe in what we cannot see because it makes us uncomfortable. Most people *really like* going about their lives, believing in what they can see and what they feel they can control. Children aren't this way, until the world, through parents, well-meaning family members, and teachers explain to them that what they are seeing (or hearing or feeling) is not real. It is the fallen world that causes unbelief–a break from the ways of God, from the truth of His creation, which includes His creation of angels.

> *"For in him all things were created: things in heaven and on earth, visible and invisible, whether thrones or powers or rulers or authorities; all things have been created through him and for him."*
> *Colossians 1:16*

The Bible says that God created even *invisible* things. What I've come to believe is this: that the things we cannot often see in the spiritual realm are more real than the things we can see in the physical. This is because the physical realm is temporal... temporary. The spiritual realm is eternal. It was, is, and will be–just as God, our creator is eternal, without beginning or end. He is not on our physical timeline but exists beyond it.

> *"Declaring the end from the beginning, and from ancient times the things that are not yet done, saying, My counsel shall stand, and I will do all my pleasure:"*
> *Isaiah 46:10 KJV*

I believe that God placed His angels (we will talk about Satan and his angels in a later chapter) on this earth to protect each one of His children from the day they are born, until the day that each one of us meet Him again in the transition from the physical realm to the spiritual realm of eternal life.

> *"For he shall give his angels charge over thee, to keep thee in all thy ways."*
> *Psalm 91:11 KJV*

My Whole Hearted Testimony

So God gave Fred charge over me. When I was little, I accepted that fact innocently. He was my companion. I distinctly remember sitting with him and talking with him. I'm sure I did all the talking, but he was a very good listener! Then I began to grow up and people told me that it wasn't okay to have an imaginary friend, so I stopped talking to Fred. Eventually I stopped seeing Fred with my eyes. But I do not believe that he ever left my side.

Today, I again know and accept that Fred is always with me. Even as I write this right now, I feel his presence over my left shoulder. He likes to be close to me. We have a special bond you see! I've had many dreams of Fred where I can see Him. His role in these dreams is always as protector and guide. This is who he was created to be!

Fred, like Jesus, and like God, has seen me through the good and the bad times–through every time of every experience in my life. I'm a child of God, precious in His sight, just like you. If what I am sharing is true, then that means that you too have an angel that God has given charge over you, for your whole life.

Step of Faith:

Here is a challenge for you: I encourage you to pray and ask the Lord to reveal to you one thing that only He knows about you. Is there something that He could show you about yourself that would bless you, the way Him showing me the *spirit cat* blessed me?

If you have never seen your angel, ask the Lord to reveal to you where it is right now! Ask the Lord to share with you your angel's name! If you want to learn more about your angel, ask the Lord to give you a dream about it.

Our God is a good, good Father and delights in blessing His children. As we seek the truth of His Kingdom, you can believe that He will generously share those truths. It is Satan who wants to keep us blind to the truth of Our Creator and His creation. It is Jesus Christ who came (and will come again!) to set you free into the fullness of who you were created to be, and the fullness of His Kingdom, which is so very near.

My Whole Hearted Testimony

CHAPTER 2: I Created All Things... Good

"God saw all that he had made, and it was very good." Genesis 1:31a

As the saying goes, "My life has not been all sunshine and roses." I say that somewhat in jest, recognizing that most of us experience less than what we would call an "easy" life. As a young child, my parents fought all the time, mostly about money or the lack thereof. My dad was a blue -collar laborer with a high school education. He was warm-hearted, easy -going, and loved kids. He worked at a meat-packing plant when my parents were first married. He would hold many different jobs from painting to line work in manufacturing. My mom had higher aspirations for her life than living in the small town she had grown up in. She pieced together a college education and eventually got a computer job working in a larger city about forty-five miles away.

On weekends, they both liked to go downtown to the local bar and drink way too much. This almost always led to fighting. One fight in particular stands out to me: I was perhaps seven or eight years old at the time. It was pretty late at night when my sisters and I awoke to the sound of screaming. I remember coming down the stairs hearing my parents yelling at each other. As I rounded the corner, I saw my mom and dad physically fighting up against a wall in the dining room. In that moment, all security was lost. I was frantic and did the only thing I thought to do: I got to the kitchen where our one phone hung on the wall. I dialed up the number to my grandparents. Through tears I explained to my Grandma that my mom and dad were hurting each other. It wasn't long, as they lived only blocks away, that my dad's parents came into the house and began breaking up the fight.

As an adult, I've come to understand that parents just do the best they can. That is all they can do. And people who have been hurt tend to hurt other people. Both of my parents experienced hurts in their lives that were not resolved, either through forgiveness or repentance. My mom's own hurt often came out as anger towards others, especially her children. She used to dig her long fingernails into the inside of my upper arm, and did the same thing to my sisters. This would happen any time we got out of line while out in public. No one else could see when she would grab my arm what she was doing. The only sign would come if I cried out, which I learned not to do as it caused her to dig deeper as she leaned down to tell me to *zip it.*

I was told all the while I grew up what a bad kid I was. My mom would tell me that I was just a brat who never listened. She would tell me that I was worthless, and even that I was a mistake. My dad rarely stood up for me or my sisters, probably because he too was afraid of my mom's temper. (Now I can say that I don't believe that is how my mom really felt about me or my sisters. Her words came from a place of her own deep pain and sorrow.)

It was Christmas Eve in the mid-80's. We had one bathroom in our house on the main floor. Everyone was needing to get ready all at once. My older sister had gotten into an argument with my mom and so she had locked herself in the bathroom. My mom ordered my dad to knock the door down, which he did reluctantly. It was literally a knockdown, drag-out fight between my sister and mom, but our fellow church congregants were none the wiser when just minutes later we arrived at the special service with pretend smiles on our faces. That was what you were supposed to do, right? The world tells us that we have to pretend that everything is just fine. We aren't hurting. We aren't broken. Everything is perfectly fine. Do we think that we can hide our broken lives from God the way we hide them from our church friends?

I can tell you right now that I was an *extremely willful child.* I know that even in the best of circumstances, I would not have been an easy child to raise. I was full of boundless energy during my waking hours. I literally never sat still. I didn't know how to! I was naturally curious, desiring to understand how things worked. I was very talkative and really wanted people to listen to me as I thought I had a lot of important things to say. Though I have always had a soft heart, I've also been bossy and manipulative trying to get other people to do what I wanted. As a child, I was a leader that no one wanted to follow! I didn't know that God wanted to be my protector, so I tried to protect myself through anger, manipulation, control, and many other sinful behaviors.

I received more than my fair share of spankings. As I got older, I graduated from the utensils in the kitchen drawer, to the inch-thick square yard stick. This was effective when applied over my back side, until one day when I had decided that I had had enough. I remember very clearly deciding that I was not going to cry this time. This played out in our laundry room as I bent over the folding table. My mom drew her arm back and swung as hard as she could and made contact. I laughed. She would not be deterred. She hit me again, and I laughed again. This went on for some time until the yard stick actually broke. I laughed. She stepped away in obvious frustration, with her anger spent. I walked slowly upstairs to my bedroom, closed the door, and lied down on my stomach on my bed. The laughter turned to tears as I poured out my pain into my pillow.

At some point in the many time-outs I experienced in my bedroom, I began to believe that there was something wrong with me. Correction: I **knew** there was something wrong with me. Why couldn't I be good? Why were my mom and dad always mad at me? Why did it feel like the people around me were always disappointed in me? Why wasn't I loved?

I made a vow in my heart that I would try to be what people wanted me to be. I chose to turn away from who I was, believing that the fullness of who I was was not good enough. I believed that I was not good. I did not know, despite my many Sunday school lessons, that God created all things and said that they were good. He said that I was good... but I did not have an understanding of that. It felt like everyone around me whom I cared and loved for was telling me that I was bad. So I began to believe them, and I began to try to change to fit what others said was "good".

Even as young girl, I began to recognize the things that the world said were good. I started to care how I looked. Up until this time in my life, I was a total tomboy. I hated to brush my hair and my teeth! I didn't care about my clothes or how I looked in them. Desiring to receive love and acceptance from others, I started to care. So that I would look better in my clothes, I started sucking in my tummy. Everywhere I went, I would suck in my tummy so that it looked flat. I began to watch what I would eat so that I wouldn't get too chubby.

These changes were subtle at first, but as I grew into my teens, the changes became more profound. I began to operate as a perfectionist— not only in my appearance, but in every area of my life.

When I was nine or ten, my parents separated. This was probably a blessing because their fighting had only escalated in frequency and severity. My mom's drinking had gotten worse, while at the same time my dad had stopped drinking, recognizing that it was a problem. My mom began to stay away from home more and more.

At this stage in my life, I was acting more like a parent than a child. I had taken responsibility, whether I was asked to our not, for raising my younger sister, Greta. I would get her ready for school in the mornings, making sure we both made it to school on time. I would walk her home after school and fix us both a snack and supper. My dad was pretty absent at this time, likely nursing his own wounds of abandonment from my mom. Around this same time, my mom lost her grandma, who was her biggest fan, and her dad, whom she had always been close to. These deaths seemed to push my mom over the edge. I can see her very clearly, even today, sitting in the high-backed chair in the corner of our dark living room, holding her head as she cried into her own hands, a moment etched in time in this little girl whose world was so uncertain.

I will never forget the day that my dad packed a bag and walked out the door. There was nothing special about the day, other than that it marked my life, as in 'before this day' and 'after this day'. I saw my dad walking down the hallway between the kitchen and living room. I was standing on the steps. When I saw that he had a suitcase in his hands, I ran to him as fast as I could and grabbed onto his pant legs. I begged him to stay. I could see the tear stains on his face. He shook me off and I slumped to the ground. He walked out the door as my mind raced. Where would he go? Would he ever come back? Would he still be my dad? What could I have done differently so that he would stay?

The time came when my parents sat all three of us daughters down to tell us that they were getting a divorce. I didn't fully understand what this would mean, but I knew that my life was only getting more out of control. Finding something good about my life in that moment would have been hard to do. Despite my best efforts of trying to be what my parents wanted me to be, my world was falling apart. And where was God in all that? Where had He gone? Because I couldn't feel Him and I couldn't see Jesus anymore. If He was a good God, surely He would protect me from this pain and uncertainty.

But God doesn't say that all things in this life are going to *feel* good. He says that all things work together for good.

> *"And we know that all things work together for good to them that love God, to them who are called according to his purpose."*
> *Romans 8:28*

I felt like I must **not** have been called according to His purpose then, because my life was not good. My life was a mess, and it was only going to get more messy! The truth is that what I was feeling, a huge part of this generation is feeling right now: Families are broken. Parents aren't parenting. Children feel abandoned and alone. I am not overstating the reality to say that billions of children and adults feel just as alone as I did in that day. But that doesn't change the fact that God is still with them, just as He was with me. He was with me in every moment and he caught every tear. I just didn't know it.

I believed the lies that the world, under Satan, was telling me (and that he has told you)–that I was alone, that I was a mistake, that I was not loved, and that all the bad things going on in my life were my fault.

You might have asked yourself before: why does God allow bad things to happen to good people? I was just a kid and didn't deserve the verbal or emotional abuse I grew up in. I deserved to have two parents working together in my life who loved me and raised me to know that I was loved, not for what I did but for who I was.

The hard truth is this: God will never force Himself on anyone. Because my parents were not in relationship with God, through His son Jesus, they were not following His ways. They were not listening to what His plan was for their life, or mine. In reality, because of their own brokenness, they were listening to the ways of the world, their flesh, and Satan —which is all twisted and broken.

My life was not going to get better, at least for a while. We had to sell our house and most of our things. We had a big sale and rented the small community center downtown. I recall seeing all of our worldly possessions on display for all to see. We didn't have a lot, but what we had was being taken away.

I didn't realize it on the day of the sale, but something very precious to me was sold: Several years before, my dad had made all three of his daughters matching doll beds. They were similar but each one was unique in the way he fashioned the wood. I knew that it must have taken him quite some time to cut, fasten, sand, and stain each one. The year I had received this gift had been my very favorite Christmas. Each of us received a small McDonald's stuffed animal in our little hand-made baby beds. This doll bed represented stability and innocence to me. That Christmas was a happy one, a time to be cherished. The one item that represented that time to me was sold for pennies.

We moved to a tiny, little, yellow one-bedroom house for a while, where I had to share a bed and bedroom with my little sister. Within a year, my mom would get remarried to a man named David who lived near Sioux City, the town where my mom worked, and we would move into his small two-bedroom house out in the country. My older sister would stay with our dad for her senior year of high school. He would meet a woman named Sandy, who had experienced her own pain and anguish, causing seeds of deep mistrust in others. A wedge was firmly planted between my dad and his daughters. My dad would never again be an active part of my life.

One highlight of my middle-school years came when I created the opportunity for myself to go to Space Camp. A number of my classmates had signed up as a part of our TAG (Talented and Gifted) class. I actually tricked my mom into attending the informational meeting. I got her to drive the ten miles to the middle school, telling her it was for a required all-parents meeting. Boy was she surprised when my teacher, Mrs. Gullikson, began sharing the details of the upcoming trip to Huntsville, Alabama... and the COSTS. My mom glared at me for much of the presentation. When it was finally over, she absolutely lost it on me on the way out to the car. She screamed at me, "Where do you think we are going to get $500 to send you to space camp?" I didn't know, but the idea came to me that I could ask my Grandma Ardis, who had always been in my corner.

I went to my Grandma with a *proposal* that I would clean her house and perform chores until the money was worked off. She agreed, and she held me to every dollar of the agreement, but I got to go to Space Camp in Huntsville, Alabama for one week that summer! This once-in-a-lifetime experience included getting to fly in airplanes, stay in dorms on campus at NASA, meet real astronauts, learn all about flight outside our atmosphere, and ride in all kinds of simulators.

In my high school years, who I was created to be would become quite lost in my quest for popularity. I did everything I could to be liked by others, continuing to honor my vow to earn love by being and doing what other people wanted. As I sit here today, I can see quite clearly how the identity God had given me had become lost as it was buried deep inside of me. I strived for perfection in my grades, needing all my teachers to see my value as a smart and gifted student. I strived to be the peace-maker with my friends, desperately wanting to be who they wanted me to be.

Lifted Up

The short amount of time I was home each day was spent quietly alone, trying to avoid any confrontations with my mom who continued to have a short fuse and a self-focus.

Boys. Ugh. I didn't have anyone to tell me that I was beautiful on the inside and that that was what counted. Instead, I heard the message loud and clear that to be liked, I needed to be perfect—which I could never hope to be. I literally grew 5 inches in one summer between my 7th and 8th grade year. I was all arms and legs, totally gangly and uncoordinated. By the time I was a freshman, I was still about ten pounds under weight and had just barely entered puberty. There was nothing curvy about me, except my backside, which my sisters compassionately referred to as a "bubble-butt". I was overly conscious of my appearance, comparing myself to senior girls who seemed to have the perfect figures.

All the popular girls in my class had "boyfriends". I knew nothing of what this even meant, but did my best to learn every stupid thing my friends shared from their so-called *vast* experience. I thought that everyone was kissing, so I should too. My first kiss was with a boy named Brad, whom I thought resembled Tom Cruise in *Top Gun*, a popular movie around that time. The kiss was terrible. Yuck! I was not at all ready to be kissing anybody but I succumbed to the peer pressure. As a sophomore, it wasn't long until I got the attention of a senior boy named Curt. Of course, kissing wasn't enough for this *man* who expected me to give him more than that. I felt so out of my league. I desperately wanted to feel love as I wasn't receiving love from my dad, who was basically out of my life, nor from my mom, who was busy attending to the dramas in her own life. Because we had moved, my grandparents, who had been a stabilizing factor in my life, were no longer nearby to guide me and hold me in their arms.

I was a part of a church youth group during this season in my life, but not to grow in a deeper relationship with the Lord. I did it out of responsibility. I didn't engage or try to build relationships with the other kids who attended, because they weren't considered popular...

My Whole Hearted Testimony

And popularity was the most important thing to me. I needed to feel accepted. I needed people to make me feel like I mattered. But I was such a fake at that time in my life. I pretended to like things other people liked. I pretended to be someone I wasn't all the time. It was truly exhausting. Of course, I went out for every sport and extra-curricular activity from basketball and track to speech and choir. Busyness became my savior. If I was busy, I didn't have time to think about things or to feel what was going on in my heart. I believe that it was at this time in my life that Satan successfully coached me into severing the connection between my head and my heart. It was like I lost the ability to understand how I was even feeling or why. I didn't cry often, and if I did, I wouldn't even know why.

During the summer between my sophomore and junior years, I met a boy named Joel. He had actually been a senior when I was a freshman but I don't think he had ever noticed me. He was the Homecoming King and Student Body President. He was Mr. Popular then. I would have thought he was out of reach to me, but by the time I was fifteen, I had grown into my 5'9 body and was more appealing to the opposite sex. His ex-girlfriend, Shannon and my ex-boyfriend, Curt, had begun to date, and so we came together to commiserate in our circumstances.

Joel would be *my first everything*. He would be my first love. He would be my first lover. He would be my first true heart-break. And I would put him first, before everything else in my life, including before my faith. We would date for nine years, off and on, only apart when he would cheat on me, coming back together when I would forgive him, believing that I could change him. My life during those years was measured by this one relationship. I became completely co-dependent upon him. If he loved me, then I was okay. If he didn't love me, then I was broken. My already malnourished faith life died completely. How could I 'live' in sin and still believe that God loved me? I couldn't, and so eventually in my shame and guilt, I convinced myself that there was no God.

Joel was 6'3 and very athletic and strong. He was hard-working and had a ton of friends. His parents were affluent and so he had lots of fun toys.

His dad owned a 2nd generation gravel pit with an A-frame house in the middle that was party central in the summer months. My friends and I loved to ride the jet skis and to go boating. There was just something about Joel that drew me to him. Call it chemistry if you want because our relationship was built on physical attraction more than anything. The problem was that Joel was not just attracted to me, and for some reason the numerous other girls that were attracted to him were not to be deterred by our so-called "monogamous" relationship. Joel literally cheated on me more times than I can count and probably more than I ever found out about.

I can see now that God did bring good people into my life to help to shape me during those critical developmental years. I had some amazing teachers in high school who invested in me from their own hearts. My biology teacher was named Mr. Wilmot. He was a goofy kind of guy who liked to say "Good afternoon" if you greeted him in the morning. I got to spend two summers working with him to make extra money. He had me help him with wiring in the school building. I knew that he saw something in me that I could not see at the time myself. He didn't look at my outsides, but he could see the mind that was growing inside of me.

God used another teacher named Mrs. Banks, my TAG teacher, to draw out of me the creativity He had placed inside my heart. It was in her classroom that I could go into a safe place, beyond the expectations of others for me, and explore the gifts I carried. I was able to creatively write and draw or paint. I didn't know it then, but seeds were planted during this time that would grow in the years ahead.

I was given many opportunities to shine. I skillfully played clarinet and did well in band contests. I had a nice voice, though not a soloist's. I got to be part of musicals in supporting roles. I did well at Speech contests and got to go to State for improvisation. I was on the varsity basketball team as a Junior and got to start as a Senior, less for my skill and more because of my height.

My Whole Hearted Testimony

My life seemed to fall apart again in my Junior year of high school when my mom and step-dad, David, got divorced because he had cheated on her and was choosing the other woman. The irony of that was that my mom had cheated on my own dad with David. Again, my mom faced devastating heartbreak that couldn't help but affect her parenting.

During my Senior year, I applied to be a Page in the Iowa House of Representatives and was chosen. I got to move down to Des Moines for two months and work in the Journal Room, helping to produce the daily periodical record. During my time in Des Moines, my mom gave birth to my brother, Lucas. She had inadvertently become pregnant by a man named Rob, whom she married just a few months before Luke was born. Rob moved in with us and overnight I had another father figure in my life. He was a nice-enough guy. Truth be told, he later confessed to me that I intimidated him. I was quite assertive, on the verge of being aggressive. I had become absolutely judgmental of others.

I had created a standard in my own mind for everyone and everything: If someone didn't meet that standard, I let them know it. I said what I thought. I had become masterful at manipulating people by then. I steered clear of my mom, who was completely wrapped up in her own life becoming a mother of a newborn at age 43.

Upon high school graduation, I received many scholarships that helped me to go to college at the University of Nebraska—Lincoln. I started out as a Communications major but I just didn't feel like it was a good fit. It didn't seem challenging enough. Joel's brother was in the Engineering college at the time. He was always a real jerk to me, but he was smart and I respected him. I went over to the Engineering school and looked through the brochures. The only pamphlet that mentioned people was Industrial Engineering, so I picked that one and enrolled for my second semester.

The summer after my freshman year of college, I moved back in with my mom and Rob to work at the local swimming pool as a head lifeguard with a close friend from high school, Teresa, who would become a roommate at Nebraska U in the fall for my Sophomore year. We both decided to try out for the Sioux City Rivercade Queen of the River competition.

As a little girl, my mom would drive us down to Sioux City to watch the Rivercade parade. I remember watching the pretty girls riding down the road in convertibles, waving to the crowds, mesmerized by their beautiful dresses and big hair. Truth be told, I signed up for the contest primarily for the college scholarship they gave to the two princesses and queen that were selected, but I figured it would be fun too to get to be one of those girls waving in the parade.

I submitted my application and waited anxiously for the preliminary judging, which was held at a hotel banquet hall one afternoon. Both Teresa and I were excited to learn later that night that both of us had been selected to be a part of the second and final phase of the competition, which would take place the week of Rivercade held in July.

The second phase began with the parade and lasted several days, filled with interviews by the judges, impromptu speaking, recreational activities, and evening concerts where the candidates were observed interacting with each other. Yes, I got to ride in the parade! My mom made a beautiful pink satin gown with a white tuxedo-style collar for me to wear. A grey Corvette was selected for me to ride in. I got to wave at all the little girls who sat along the edge of the street on the parade route. It was a pretty amazing experience.

The pageant itself culminated in a banquet and "crowning" of the Queen and her court. My mom, Rob, Joel, and my grandparents attended to support me. To my surprise, I was selected as one of the two princesses. My friend, Teresa, was not chosen, but she was a very good sport about it. Over the next year, I would attend more local parades than I could count. I'm sure that I mastered "the wave". I know that my cheek muscles got a workout from all that smiling that was required along the miles and miles of parade route. This experience was a wonderful blessing to me, and a highlight of that period of my life.

My Whole Hearted Testimony

I lived with Teresa for my Sophomore year of college in the same apartment complex as Joel. I'm certain that I wanted to live close to him just to try to control him more to keep him from cheating on me. Looking back now, it was such a toxic relationship but my heart just would not let go of the hope that someday he would learn to love me the way I thought I loved him.

At the end of that school year, he was beginning to move out of his apartment and so he was storing his computer at my place. I was using it to type a paper when I found myself reading his email not by accident but because I was drawn to it like a bee to honey. I should not have been shocked to find a long string of emails to and from another girl. The communication had gone on for months. Joel was literally seeing someone else on the side. I can still vividly remember his pounding on my door and crying out in regret outside my apartment door after I had confronted him with the evidence. He was so remorseful. I vowed to break up with him and never date him again... but that promise to myself only lasted weeks.

We got back together, again. And a year later, nearly the same scenario played out again when he was moving out of the next apartment. I was literally in the back of his pickup truck loading bricks into the truck bed that he had used in his living room around the small fireplace. A girl I had never met came up the walk way and asked for Joel. I told her where to find him inside. A little later she left while I was still laboring with the bricks. When I asked Joel about her, he acted innocent and I bought his story.

Joel moved in with a guy friend of his for the last few weeks of school. One night I went over to his friend's house to look for him and found a note from another girl on the windshield of his car. Apparently, he had gone out with her the day before and she was thanking him for the great time. I was crushed again. Rinse and repeat.

There was a time during my college years that I was so fearful of dying because I knew in my heart that I would go to hell because of my sinful

Lifted Up

choices. Though I no longer confessed a belief in God, I knew that the way I was choosing to live was wrong and that I would pay for my sin. During one of my many break-ups with Joel, I contemplated killing myself. What kept me from following through was my fear of what awaited me in death.

I also recall thinking to myself that if I screwed up the suicide, which I had pictured would come through a car accident, I would end up disfigured, unable to be of value to society, and alone.

What is it about the broken places in our heart that draw the same pain back in over and over again? The only way to stop this is for that broken place to be healed. But I didn't know that back then. I just knew that I loved Joel and that life without him would be worse than life with him even if he kept hurting me. I was carrying around a lot of shame and guilt over my choices which gave the enemy a legal right to hold me captive in my sin. I was also believing the lie that the only way to atone for my sins with him was to "make it right" in God's eyes by getting married.

I graduated with my Bachelor's Degree in Industrial & Management Systems Engineering after 5 long years. It was a blur of classes, studying for tests, working, and heart-breaks. For three of the five years, I lived with three guy friends who were great. They looked out for me. They were *low-maintenance* and there was little drama in our place, apart from what was going on with Joel. I can see God's hand in this living situation as our apartment was a place of calm in the storm.

Around this same time in my life, my new stepdad, Rob, attempted suicide due to mental and behavioral health problems. I was over at Joel's when I received a phone call from my mom, who was at the hospital with Rob. She instructed me that I was to go through the garbage at our house to search for chemicals and poisons that Rob may have ingested. Joel brought me home and helped me dig through the trash cans inside our house and outside. We found all kinds of household cleaner containers, rat poison, along with coffee grounds that he had used to brew the poisonous concoction. We drove the garbage remains to the hospital, which was located in a larger nearby city where Rob was being treated.

I distinctly remember walking down the long, narrow hospital hallway, carrying garbage sacks. A nurse met me to take the items. As I stopped to hand them to her, I looked over and saw Rob look up from the table he was perched on in an exam room across from me. There was a look of desperation in his eyes that I will never forget, but also a look of regret: I could feel his need for forgiveness calling out to me.

Mom and Rob stayed together after this, at least for a time. Rob agreed to seek treatment for his mental illness and they invested significant funds to send him to an in-patient treatment center in California for an extended period of time.

Mom and Rob ended up getting divorced, my mom's third failed marriage. Again, my mom's heart suffered greatly. She did her best to keep it together despite the incredibly difficult circumstances. She owned her own computer business by this time, and would raise Lucas on her own.

Rob passed away a few years ago naturally but unexpectedly, when Luke was in his teens, from untreated diabetes. He had continued to be on the outskirts of Luke's life as Luke grew into a teenager, but despite the distance in their relationship, the loss Lucas felt in losing his father deeply impacted him, especially at a time when he was growing into a man himself. In God's perfect plan, children grow up with the security of both their parents. A boy has his father to look to as an example of how to become a man, and a girl has her mom in the same way. But this is not the world that kids grow up in these days.

Satan absolutely loves to see children being hurt in any way possible and then acting out of that hurt place in their heart. He works without ceasing, sowing seeds of pain in every child where he has been given legal right. Who gives this legal right? The difficult answer to that question is God. God is the one who created the rules. He gave Adam and

Eve free will. Satan tempted them and they chose disobedience in eating the apple of the knowledge of good and evil. Satan was then given a seat at the table to each person's life.

That does not mean that it is God's heart that His children would be hurt. **It is never God's heart that any of us would be hurt.** Here is the good news: Satan does not have a blank check. Yes, he roams around seeking whom he would devour (1 Peter 5:8), but he cannot cause us to sin unless we choose to follow him. And God gives us every opportunity to turn away from sin. He gave us His word, the Bible, to be our guide as it lays out for us an understanding of who God is and His ways. It is clear about what to do and what not to do, in order to avoid sin causing pain to ourselves or others. Even greater than that, He gave us His Son, the Word made flesh, sent to live on this earth as a man, demonstrating life without sin, but taking on all of our sin on His own shoulders at the cross.

When we are in the middle of heartache, it can be very difficult to see God's hand moving, but we can trust that it is. His hand is always moving in our life, bringing good out of the worst of situations. I can now look back over the four decades of my life and see the way the Lord has redeemed every challenge, every mistake, every deep hurt for His purposes. Because He has called me by name, I am His. Even when I chose to turn away from Him, He never turned from me. He never stopped pursuing me, and **He will never stop pursuing you**. We are His most precious creation, created for a purpose – relationship with Him. There is nothing we could ever do that He would cause Him to stop loving us. He is not like our own mom or dad. His love is not conditional. I know and feel the truth deep within me that God has used every situation in my life to bring me closer to Him. Only God can bring good from the bad.

The other key thing to recognize as we live out our lives, hopefully working to be in alignment with God's purposes and not Satan's, is this: Vengeance is not ours. God calls us to forgive every person who has hurt us, no matter the offense. Just as he forgives us for every sin and mistake when we repent, each person has that same opportunity, no matter what they have done. But if they should not repent, that is God's business and not our own. When we choose to forgive, we receive freedom. When we repent of our sin, we receive freedom. But what happens if someone hurts us and will not ask for forgiveness? Well, Satan would have us believe that it *is only fair* that we should hurt them back. But that is not the way of God. Here is a parable Jesus shares:

Then Jesus told his disciples a parable to show them that they should always pray and not give up. ² He said: "In a certain town there was a judge who neither feared God nor cared what people thought. ³ And there was a widow in that town who kept coming to him with the plea, 'Grant me justice against my adversary.'

⁴ "For some time he refused. But finally he said to himself, 'Even though I don't fear God or care what people think, ⁵ yet because this widow keeps bothering me, I will see that she gets justice, so that she won't eventually come and attack me!'"

⁶ And the Lord said, "Listen to what the unjust judge says. ⁷ And will not God bring about justice for his chosen ones, who cry out to him day and night? Will he keep putting them off? ⁸ I tell you, he will see that they get justice, and quickly. However, when the Son of Man comes, will he find faith on the earth?"

Luke 18:1-8

What is Jesus saying here? I believe that he was trying to help His disciples understand that their job is to petition their Judge, Father God, for justice and leave it in His capable hands. Jesus said that God will see that His people get justice. It may not happen when and how they want, but it will happen at the end of this age, when each of us will be called to account for our thoughts, words, and deeds.

Vengeance is not ours.

It is God's. Period.

My Whole Hearted Testimony

Declaration of Faith: (Pray aloud)

Father, God, you know how I have been hurt. You know every wound that I have received at the hands of others, and even because of my own actions. Lord, you also know every sin that I have committed. Yet, I know that you have never turned away from me. You have been with me through every time of joy, and every time of sorrow. You are the God of the universe, vast and mighty, and also the God of my heart, intimately aware of every facet of my existence.

I ask forgiveness for every sin, for every hurt that I have caused. I also choose to forgive every trespass against me. I place it all at the foot of the cross covered in Jesus' blood, fully forgiven and severed from my life. I declare today a freedom from my past. What I have done and what I have experienced is not who I am. I declare my love for you, and that I have been called according to your purposes. I accept with my whole heart that you work all things together for my good. Amen.

CHAPTER 3: In the End... I Will Come for My Bride

After college, I went to work for a company called Pella, a manufacturer of windows and doors. They were building a new plant near my home town in Iowa so I was able to move back to Akron, where I had attended High School and where Joel was living. I didn't appreciate it at the time, but Pella was founded and operated on sound Christian principles of mutual respect and doing the right thing. During work hours, I was surrounded by Godly men and women, people who cared about other people and treated me well. I found some "solid ground" for the first time in many years. I flourished as I was given opportunities to problem-solve and lead others.

I took up the hobby of motorcycles, purchasing my first bike—a Harley Davidson Sportster 883. It was purple with flames and Screaming Eagle exhaust pipes. This allowed me entrance into the "guys' club" of riding. There were many men at the plant whom I worked with who had motorcycles and enjoyed riding together. My favorite part of riding a motorcycle was feeling the wind in my hair. It felt a lot like flying!

I began to enjoy life again, as I wasn't operating only out of survival mode. I saved up to buy my first house. I decided to move away from Akron, where Joel lived and where I had been renting a small apartment from his parents, to a town called LeMars about twenty miles away. I can see now the way God was helping me to pull away from this unhealthy relationship little by little. My first house was a little yellow two-bedroom single story house built in the 50's. I liked the challenge of updating the house, figuring out how to refinish flooring and cabinets, replace light and plumbing fixtures, wallpaper, paint, and decorate to make the house into a home.

My relationship with Joel became more and more dysfunctional. There was no trust left between us. I knew there must be more to life than what I was experiencing. Real love continued to evade me. I was as lonely and dissatisfied as ever, despite some professional success that I was experiencing. I believe it was the Lord working in my life, though I did not know it at the time, who gave me the strength to apply for a job with Pella out on the East Coast in Pennsylvania. The company had just built a plant in Gettysburg, PA.

I flew out of Omaha and into the Baltimore airport the weekend prior to September 11th, 2001. My interview went well and I was told to expect an offer the following week. I looked at houses over the weekend and had time to visit the Hershey's Chocolate plant, as well as make the short trip to Washington D.C. to see the major monuments and land-marks on Monday, September 10th.

On 9/11, I departed Baltimore on an early morning flight. We had a layo-ver in St. Louis, on our way back to Omaha. We were asked to de-plane while they cleaned the plane. When it was time to re-board, I found my new seat and waited patiently for others to board. It was at this time that the pilot came over the plane's PA to tell us that there had been a major accident in New York City and all planes in the U.S. were being grounded for a period of time. We were asked to get back off the plane to wait in the terminal.

I remember hurriedly walking through the vast terminal looking for a television. I found a large group of people huddled around one in an open bar & restaurant. We stood there together watching the aftermath on the screen of the planes that hit the World Trade Center in New York City. As I stood there watching, the first tower fell.

Everyone was shocked and there was so much speculation about what had happened. Was it just a bad accident? Had we been attacked? What was going to happen next? Very soon after that, an announce-ment was made over the Terminal PA stating that the airport had been ordered to close.

Immediately, I realized that I did not have a Plan B. I had a couple of dol-lars in my pocket, having spent all the cash I had taken on my trip over the weekend. I went looking for an ATM only to find that of course there had been a run on funds and so it was empty. The cell phone I carried had only a small charge left on it. I went to make a call to my family to let them know that I was okay, but the cell phone network was out of service, probably due to so much volume all at once.

Quickly, I decided that I would try to rent a car since St. Louis wasn't terribly far from Omaha. I followed the crowds heading out the main doors of the terminal, looking for the signs to guide me to the rental car stations. I had only a small bag on me. My luggage wasn't released that day in the rush of things, but would show up a week later in Sioux Falls, SD, where I would have to drive to retrieve it.

I made it onto a shuttle bus, taking me off the main airport grounds to the rental car company buildings. I was dropped at one of the buildings and commenced to standing in the long queue for my turn at the counter. When it was finally my turn, I walked forward. The rental car representative asked me for my ID. I handed over my driver's license and was told almost immediately that I was not old enough to rent a car. What? I was twenty-four years old, but apparently that did not make the cut at this rental car business. I was pretty shaken at this point.

I had no money. My phone did not work. I had no car, and I knew no one. So, I just started walking. I found my way from the rental car yards to the Interstate. It wasn't too long and a car pulled over next to me to offer me a ride. There were two young men in the car dressed nicely and I assumed they were businessmen. Here I was, this attractive young woman, walking by myself in the middle of the morning on the Interstate.

Yes, I believe God's hand was working in my life on that morning!
These two men offered me a ride. I happily accepted, without hesitation, as I had no other plan. I learned that they had also been kicked out of the airport following the planes hitting the Trade Center. Their company had cars available and so they were able to borrow a company car. They weren't able to take the car out of the city but they offered to bring me to the train station. That sounded like a good plan to me so off we went.

They found the train station. As we approached, I think they feared for my safety. There were all kinds of "unsavory" types out front. We pulled up only to be told that the train station had closed as well. We were directed to the Greyhound Bus Station which wasn't too far away, still in the same run down and dilapidated neighborhood of St. Louis. They found the Bus Station and I hopped out, thanking them kindly for the ride.

The Bus Station was full of people. Tensions were running high, due to the uncertainty of what had happened and what was still transpiring. I went to the counter and was able to purchase a one-way ticket from St. Louis to Kansas City departing later in the afternoon. I was also able to use a pay phone, calling my family who knew that I had been out on the east coast, even in Washington D.C. the day before. They were relieved that I was safe. I also got in touch with a sweet lady at the Pella plant named Sue. She became my lifeline that day, reassuring me that Pella would do whatever they needed to do ensure that I got home safely, since we weren't certain that the buses would actually be allowed to run with events continuing to play out. (Each year on the anniversary of 9/11, her and I exchange well-wishes acknowledging the bond that that day forged between us.)

There were tiny TVs mounted on chairs that you could plug a quarter into to watch for a few minutes. People were taking turns plugging the quarters so that we could watch the news for updates. We learned that not only had there been an attack in New York City, but that other planes were involved in Washington D.C. at the Pentagon, which I had driven by the day before, as well as in Pennsylvania.

The events of that fateful day are forever etched in my mind. Thankfully, my bus was allowed to run and I made it as far as Kansas City late that night, where my sister, Molly, came to pick me up. She drove me back to Omaha, where I collapsed on her couch. The next morning Joel came to pick me up to drive me back to northwest Iowa. I went back to work, but life did not go back to normal for me, or for anyone else.

Lifted Up

9/11 changed things—for everyone. The safety we had taken for granted in America was no longer guaranteed. The acts of terrorism were successful in creating terror.

In the weeks ahead, I did not receive a job offer to the plant in Pennsylvania. The housing market began to fall, which negatively impacted the production of the plant and the plans for the start-up. It turns out, I was not meant to move to the East Coast. God had other plans for me!

A number of months later, I received a call from an engineer named Chris working at a Pella plant in Portland, Oregon. They were still expanding their operations and were looking for an engineer with my skill set. Within a couple of weeks, I had flown out there to interview, and had a job offer. I told Joel that either he was going to have to ask me to marry him, or I was moving to the West Coast. He said he wasn't ready for marriage, so I sold my house in Iowa, and bought a new condo in Vancouver, WA just across the bridge from Portland, only minutes from the plant I would be working at.

I moved in July of 2002. I didn't know another soul. My loneliness reached new levels. The highlight of my week was the Netflix movies that were delivered on Friday afternoon to give me something to do over the weekend. My mom and I had had a major fight before I moved, and so she was not in my life at all during this season. I liked my job and the people at the plant, but my existence was empty. I again relied upon my own performance to help me to feel some value in my hollow life.

I signed up to start my MBA at Portland State in the fall. I also inquired of the little airfield in the middle of Vancouver. I had taken a couple of flying lessons in Iowa prior to moving, and picked that back up, taking flight school and spending a $100 per hour for lessons. I had sold my motorcycle prior to purchasing my first house, so flying became my new hobby of choice. Over the next three years I would log 100 hours of flight time, though I would not receive my official pilot's license. I soloed in a "tail-dragger" airplane known as a J-3 Cub.

My Whole Hearted Testimony

The main pilot sat in the back seat of the two-seater. A long pole came up through the bottom between the pilot's legs and acted as the main hand controls.

I am convinced there is nowhere prettier than the land I got to fly over in Washington and Oregon at an altitude of 2,000 to 4,000 feet. The plane was open so that the only barrier between the occupants and the sky was a small windshield. It literally felt like I was flying the airplane with my arms flapping up and down!

It was during this season of supreme loneliness and striving that I finally came to the end of myself and gave my life *back* to the Lord.

(A few days before this in September 2002, Joel had broken up with me for the last time. There was nothing I could do to keep us together. Apparently he needed 'companionship' and he found someone else to meet those needs closer to home. I had made my choice to move away, and that was that.)

It was a Saturday morning. I went for a run, which I would commonly do. On my way back to my condo located inside a gated community, I just broke down sobbing. I felt more alone in this one moment in my life than ever before, and that was saying something. I remember looking up at my place, which was on the second floor. I thought to myself: how had this become my whole life? I made it back to my place and went in to take a shower. While in the shower, I continued to cry. I cried and cried, and eventually cried out in desperation to God:

I said, "I give up. I can't do this anymore. I've made a mess of my life. Please help me." As the water streamed down over me, I felt comforted somehow.

Later that same afternoon, I met the man who would become my fiancé just three months later and my husband within nine months. The same engineer who had gotten me the job at the Portland plant, Chris, had invited me to join him at a Husker watch-party at a local establishment.

He too was a UNL grad and a big Husker fan. I went reluctantly, knowing that it was better for me to be around other people than just wallow in my self-pity. I noticed Garrick from across the room, and later I learned that he had noticed me too! We had a short conversation that day, and we saw each other again the following week at the same place for another game. We exchanged numbers and began talking regularly. I know now that Garrick saw something in me that Joel was never meant to see. For nine years, I had tried to force my own will. I tried everything in my power for Joel to love me, when he was never meant to. Now I know that God had created someone else for Joel, and he had created me for Garrick, to be his partner in this life.

It was a whirlwind romance. Garrick truly swept me off my feet, complete with love poems and romantic gestures of every kind. He treated me with honor and respect. He showed me what it was to feel cherished. I believe that God caused Garrick to fall head over heels in love with me.

Maybe that sounds silly or doesn't fit your doctrine that God would do that, but here is why I believe this: because Garrick had been hurt in every way imaginable in his young life and into adulthood. He had not dated much because of his broken heart, and he was extremely guarded. Garrick falling for me at that time was not a part of his own plan. He had a group of close friends that meant the world to him, and he loved his job. He had just bought his first place, a brownstone in Beaverton, Oregon. He had two male roommates who were his best friends. He wasn't looking for me, and yet there I was.

On the other hand, it was equally supernatural, that I was able to let go of the strong soul ties to Joel enough to be able to bond with Garrick. There were times it all felt quite surreal—all of a sudden finding myself in the arms of another man, making lifetime plans together after only weeks of meeting. I know that God must have given me the strength to walk away once and for all from the unhealthy relationship of my teen and early adult years. Garrick would tell you that I freaked out more than once, which is true. I had so many unhealthy ways of relating that needed to be healed and relearned. In fact, I am still learning to do this after more than fifteen years of marriage!

We were engaged at Christmas in 2002 at the rustic Skamania Lodge overlooking the Columbia River Gorge, where Garrick had whisked me away as a surprise. Somehow, some way, I was able to let go of my relationship with Joel that had held me firmly in its grip for so many years. The day I gave my life to the Lord He began to guide my life, with me finally not working against him. He led me directly into Garrick's path.

> *"For I know the plans I have for you," declares the* LORD, *"plans to prosper you and not to harm you, plans to give you hope and a future.* [12] *Then you will call on me and come and pray to me, and I will listen to you." Jeremiah 29:11-12*

Garrick and I were married the summer after we met, back in the town I had grown up in, Ireton, in the same Lutheran church I had been baptized and confirmed in. The wedding was everything I had ever dreamed of, though I had never pictured the groom as being this tall, dark, and handsome man from Missouri. I chose lavender and silver as our colors. I had four bridesmaids and he had four groomsmen. Garrick had chosen a small string quartet to play for us. I walked down the aisle to his outstretched arms while Canon In D played. My dad did come to the wedding and played the part of my father, walking me down the aisle. This was a special blessing to me. Though I did not feel that my dad knew me anymore, he was still my dad.

The wedding reception was held in my Grandma Ardis's back yard, complete with a big white tent and all the people I loved. She had worked hard to prepare the yard. It was so beautiful with flowers of every kind, and even a wedding arch and gate to walk through upon our arrival. A horse-drawn carriage picked us up at the church and brought us out to her home just outside of town. While we were eating from a delicious catered buffet, a gentle rain came down cleansing everything, cooling off the late June evening. Everything in that moment was perfect, truly!

The Wedding Supper that is coming:

Then I heard what sounded like a great multitude, like the roar of rushing waters and like loud peals of thunder, shouting:

"Hallelujah!
For our Lord God Almighty reigns.
⁷ Let us rejoice and be glad
and give him glory!
For the wedding of the Lamb has come,
and his bride has made herself ready.
⁸ Fine linen, bright and clean,
was given her to wear."

(Fine linen stands for the righteous acts of God's holy people.)

⁹ Then the angel said to me, "Write this: Blessed are those who are invited to the wedding supper of the Lamb!" And he added, "These are the true words of God."   Revelation 19:6-9

As wonderful as my own wedding and reception was, it will pale in comparison to what is coming when Jesus returns for *His Bride*.

You can be assured that God is the best wedding planner ever, and He will spare no expense when it comes to the party He has planned for His Son, Jesus, who will once again be reunited with His Bride—not just one woman dressed in white, but an entire people, man and woman, robed in righteousness, who have chosen to give themselves over to the Lord in all areas of their life, being made holy not through their own capabilities, but through the working of Holy Spirit in their lives.

"I will greatly rejoice in the Lord, my soul shall be joyful in my God; for he hath clothed me with the garments of salvation, he hath covered me with the robe of righteousness, as a bride-groom decketh himself with ornaments, and as a bride adorneth herself with her jewels." Isaiah 61:10 KJV

If I had had my way, and God had stopped pursuing me, leaving me to my own devices, I would have eventually married Joel and spent a life-time trying to change him, making him and myself miserable, living as someone I was never meant to be. Instead **I believe that the moment I chose to surrender to my Creator's plans for me, in His amazing grace, He began to work a plan to redeem my whole life.** Though the path I had been on was my own, He was even able to redeem those things that were not of Him, working all things for my good.

Perhaps your experience has been like mine, or maybe you've never turned away from the Lord as I had for so many years. But unless you've surrendered all your life to Him, every area, you are missing His very best for you.

The Lord has spoken to me quite a bit about the critical nature of the Bride and the preparation that is at hand. God doesn't need us and could do anything and everything without us, but He CHOOSES to work with us. The principle holds with respect to the Bride. It has always been His plan to have a people who would not only say, but live out, this statement: "He is our God and we are His people." The Bride of Christ will be His people in every way.

Here are a couple of the words God has given to me about the nature of His Bride and the work that is to be done in our hearts to be trans-formed into what He intended:

Lifted Up

March 8th, 2015 – A word from Jesus

"Honor me. Call out to me with every breath and I will give you life. You think you know my heart but you do not. You think I am with you and then I depart only to return later. I do not ever leave you or forsake you. I have taken up residence in your heart and I will never leave you. You turn away from me and don't comprehend how that hurts me.

I am the love of your very life. You are my bride but you do not ready yourself with preparations for our wedding banquet. You are so busy making everyone else a priority that you neglect me, and you neglect yourself. You are beautiful to me. You are worth every piece of gold and every precious stone that I have under heaven. Yet you look to people for worth and value. Turn away from sin and sin no more.

Rest in me. I will show you a new way. A way that will cost you everything and nothing. Oh, the plans I have for you. You can be my friend! You can walk with me in the very heaven of your heart. All that I have is yours and I am calling to you. Will you answer me? Will you have your lamp trimmed and ready at the appointed hour?

Why settle for anything less than everything God has to give you. Every good and perfect gift from above is at your fingertips. Come, dine with me. Come and rest at my feet. Come and dance with me. You are not of this world. You are not burdened by the things of this world. You are no longer chained by the enemy's lies. See him for what he is: a liar and a thief. He is nothing but a serpent under your heel, crushed by the love that I have for you and the sacrifice that has already been made for eternity for you to walk with me. I love you in a way that you cannot comprehend on this earth. My Father's love has no bounds and thus mine is just as great. Come to me now and dance with me, my bride."

My Whole Hearted Testimony

July 13th, 2015 – A word from the Lord

"My bride must ready herself. She must be so consumed in her love for me that even as everything falls around her, she hardly notices, except to share her testimony of her heart for her groom, for what he has done in her life, and for the eternal life that is hers."

"How does one ready themselves for the coming wedding feast? I call every child to humble himself and lay down his life so that I may give him a new one. I cry out to each heart that the plans I have for each person are so much greater than any plan they have comprised for themselves. One can only imagine from their own circumstances and imagination. They are bound by this earth, but I have NO BOUNDS for you.

My desire for each of My children is to bless them with every good thing. Just as a parent, My frustration comes when My children are stubborn and insist upon their own way. They leave all of My blessings sitting out in the cold rain when they close their ears to the breath of My spirit. So open your ears. Stop and rest so that you may hear My voice. Rest so that I can revive you to give you the energy you will need for the day of preparation at hand." (I then saw a picture of the business of an actual wedding day.)

"I call to a bride that is pure of heart. Purification comes through My word and My spirit and through My Son. When every sin is laid down and covered by His divine sacrifice, you are made pure. When you invite me into your heart, I can robe you in righteousness so that you may sit in heavenly places. My word is truth. Purification comes when you hear My word and take it in, when you let it guide every decision for yourselves and for those you love. The bride of Christ has no place for hard-heartedness."

"You are forgiven only as you forgive. How can I look upon you

when you hold a blemish in your heart? Every unforgiven hurt is a blemish that gets in the way. I look upon you from your mother's womb and see every detail of your life, and every choice that brings you closer or further from me. Every moment is an opportunity to be renewed.

There is truly no distance from me, since I am in you always. Yet you picture this void to exist. This chasm is a lie and I desire every heart to know the truth, the only truth that I am in you, and you are in me, and that there is no separation except through thought. Do not let thoughts get in the way. Do not allow flesh to get in the way. My bride is pure, and holy. She has been washed white as snow in the blood of the lamb. She is humble and ready to serve me. Her heart is open and without blemish. She is the picture of radiance as her beauty shines forth in the forgiveness she extends to anyone. Truth is the only thing on her lips as she speaks forth with grace and kindness."

"This is the time when the sheep are separated from the goats. Which one will you be, My people? Will you walk with me into eternity, or will you run from me now, and beg at My heels later when it is too late? The gates of hell are open, wide open. Time is so short."

Do you hear the sense of urgency in the tone of these messages? I certainly do. The reality is that time is a limited resource that will come to an end, and for each of us, we don't know when our time will expire. Jesus spoke with this same sense of urgency when he shared the Parable of the Wedding Feast in Luke 14:15-23:

When one of those at the table with him heard this, he said to Jesus, "Blessed is the one who will eat at the feast in the kingdom of God."

[16] Jesus replied: "A certain man was preparing a great banquet

and invited many guests. [17] At the time of the banquet he sent his servant to tell those who had been invited, 'Come, for everything is now ready.'

[18] "But they all alike began to make excuses. The first said, 'I have just bought a field, and I must go and see it. Please excuse me.'

[19] "Another said, 'I have just bought five yoke of oxen, and I'm on my way to try them out. Please excuse me.'

[20] "Still another said, 'I just got married, so I can't come.'

[21] "The servant came back and reported this to his master. Then the owner of the house became angry and ordered his servant, 'Go out quickly into the streets and alleys of the town and bring in the poor, the crippled, the blind and the lame.'

[22] "'Sir,' the servant said, 'what you ordered has been done, but there is still room.'

[23] "Then the master told his servant, 'Go out to the roads and country lanes and compel them to come in, so that my house will be full.

I remember as a little girl learning a song about this parable that we would sing in Sunday School. It went something like this: "I cannot come to the banquet, don't trouble me now. I have married a wife. I have bought me a cow. I have fields and commitments that cost a pretty sum. Pray, hold me excused, I cannot come." If you know this song, I am sure you are humming it now in your head. Sometimes the boys would change the words to say "I have married a cow, and I have bought me a wife." Silly boys.

Is that how you are living right now, as if all of your worldly commitments are more important than preparing for eternity? For so much of my life, that was how I lived. Now I have awareness of the urgency of time, yet I battle with my flesh to prioritize God in my life above all other things. You might question: aren't we given a life here as humans to live that life? The answer is yes, but we've bought into the lies of Satan that that means we get to choose how we live, what we do, how we spend our time, without consequences.

But there is always a cost. Yes, we get to choose. We can choose to follow God and His plan for our life, or we can choose to follow the ways of this world. Jesus said it this way in John chapter 17 verses 14 to 16:

> *"I have given them your word and the world has hated them, for they are not of the world any more than I am of the world. My prayer is not that you take them out of the world but that you protect them from the evil one. They are not of the world, even as I am not of it."*

Pray with me:

Lord, God – We thank you that you have called us by name. You have not only called us to be your servants, or even your friends, though we leap at the opportunity to be a friend of God! Beyond that, you call us sons and daughters through Jesus Christ. As such, we are given the inheritance of a King, The King. You tell us that which is yours, is ours.

The truth that you speak into our hearts even goes beyond a birthright. You give each of us the opportunity that Jesus spoke about in the parable, that no matter where we come from or what we have done, we may be invited into the Wedding Supper, not only as a guest, but as your Bride, having been made ready. Lord, teach us to lay down our own lives and our own plans to follow you. Teach us what it is to be in the world but not of it.

We ask you to do a work in our hearts so that we may be purified and made clean to be given a robe of righteousness to wear on that great and glorious day of the Wedding Supper of the Lamb as part of The Bride. Amen

CHAPTER 4: I Can Make Your Heart Whole

My marriage to Garrick has not been perfect by any means, but it has been full of joy and so many good gifts, including our four children, currently ages seven to twelve.

I was working as a Senior Plant Engineer with Pella in Macomb, Illinois when we had Zander George in 2006. I had no idea how to be a mom AND do the work I was doing at that time. I worked long hours and had a lot of responsibility with many people counting on me to keep a plant up and running. We joke that Zander was born to be in the top 1%. This is because he was born on his actual due date, which only happens about 10% of the time. My water also broke with him on the evening before he was born, which also only happens naturally about 10% of the time... hence the top 1%.

Zander is definitely our "first fruit". He was born with a kind, soft heart. He is naturally outgoing and makes friends easily. He is an explorer and risk-taker. As a toddler, we had to unscrew the lightbulbs in his room because he would get up and turn the lights on in the middle of the night. We also had to turn the lock hardware around on the door because he learned early on how to open his door. He would roam the house and make messes in the wee hours of the night, so we began locking him in his bedroom. (Don't worry, we had a two-way camera and a smoke alarm in the room in case of emergency!) We also had to remove the book shelf from his room because he would crawl out of his crib and pull all his books out of his shelf onto the floor. He was a handful! He still is, but in a very good way.

We should have recognized Zander's special heart for the Lord even earlier than we did, since his first two syllable word was "Amen", which occurred in Church one Sunday morning after the Pastor finished praying. The church was silent, except for a loud but little voice hollering out "Amen" for all to hear.

He always had and to this day has a ball in his hand. He is *all* boy. He

loves sports, especially basketball and football. Not so long ago he said to me, "Mom, I really want to play in the NFL, but if that is not what God wants for me, I will do what He wants."
He is a son after God's own heart.

This is a journal entry from **March 10th, 2014** where the Lord spoke to me about Zander.

> Today is the day The Lord hath made. I will rejoice and be glad in it. Good morning Lord. This morning, I keep hearing first fruits. All that I have is yours. Show me how I can give you my first fruits.

> *"You can give me that first thought of the day. You can give me your first child. Zander is special. I have special plans for him. You see it. You sense it. I confirm it. That anger that boils up (in him) is not for me. The enemy senses it, too. Zander is close to me. He holds me in his heart. I love him. Zander is meant for great things. Oh, how glorious it will be to see each of the children I've called worshipping and learning together. A super cell—that is what we are creating. They will be powerful in me, through me. I treasure each one. Beautiful. Lovely. Kind. Caring. Joyous. Hopeful. Imaginative. Creative. Trials in this life will be faced but their strength will come from me. I am doing something powerful. I am choosing to move at this time. You sense that power, the desire to turn the tables. I am victorious. I am."*

On **Sept. 8th, 2015**, The Lord spoke this to me about Zander:

> *"Zander brings me great joy. He is a treasure. My firstborn son among many. I am well pleased. When you look upon him, I show you that which he is becoming. No more a boy, but a man. His heart is tender and well cared for. You have done well by him. You are a good mother."*

Lifted Up

God gave me a beautiful experience dealing with Zander a few years ago, when I was seated on the edge of my bed one evening praying. I looked up towards the door to the hallway and I saw Zander walk into the bedroom. I wasn't seeing this physically but with my spiritual eyes. I knew I was seeing Zander, only he was not a young boy, but a man.

He looked like he was 21 or 22. He was at least 6'2" tall and so hand-some. His hair was the same color blond that it is today, only it framed his face differently. His face was strong yet kind. His shoulders were broad and his body had filled out and appeared chiseled. I was taking his appearance in and pondering why I would be seeing Zander in the future. Then the Lord began to talk with me about the plans He has for Zander in the years ahead, and my role in shaping his character to pre-pare him for all the things God has in store for him.

Why would God choose to show me my son as an adult now? I believe the Lord wants to give us insights about our life and the life of those we love. He does this because he wants to partner with us. God delights in sharing His heart with us so that we may know how to pray.

Not so long ago, I learned a valuable lesson. It was an epiphany really to me. For all of my prayer life, which has been off and on, cold, and rarely intense, I would come to the Lord thinking about what I needed and wanted. Then I would try to lay it out for God so that He would under-stand my point of view and get on board with what I was asking for. Does this sound familiar? Come on, be honest. Have you ever tried to convince God to give you what you wanted, believing that if you just made a good enough case, He would give in like we often do as parents with our children.

The epiphany was this – That, in the beginning, it was the words that God spoke that caused us and all of earth to come into existence. Therefore, words must matter in general, even when they come from us. I knew that the Bible instructs us to use our words wisely.

"But I tell you that everyone will have to give account on the day of judgment for every empty word they have spoken. For by your words you will be acquitted, and by your words you will be condemned."   *Matthew 12:36-37*

How much more when we bring our words to Him directly? Taking that thinking a step further, God created me and has a perfect plan for my life and for each person I love. He brings good out of every situation. Instead of praying out of my own flesh, which is inherently selfish, or praying from my own mind which has a limited view point, what if I could learn to pray *FROM* God's own heart? This could change everything!

Instead of "calling up" God when I have a free 5 minutes to relay to Him my list of demands, what if, first of all, I could learn to keep the connection "open" so that I never "hung up" on God? Could I learn to always keep one ear trained on God, while going about my day, interacting with people and doing the work in front of me? Is it possible for us to hear from God at all times so that we know His viewpoint on any situation? Well, I believe the answer is that yes, this is possible, though I am still trying to learn to consistently do this for myself.

"As for you, you were dead in your transgressions and sins, [2] in which you used to live when you followed the ways of this world and of the ruler of the kingdom of the air, the spirit who is now at work in those who are disobedient. [3] All of us also lived among them at one time, gratifying the cravings of our flesh and following its desires and thoughts. Like the rest, we were by nature deserving of wrath. [4] But because of his great love for us, God, who is rich in mercy, [5] made us alive with Christ even when we were dead in transgressions—it is by grace you have been saved.

[6] And God raised us up with Christ and seated us with him in the heavenly realms in Christ Jesus, [7] in order that in the coming ages he might show the incomparable riches of his grace, expressed in

Lifted Up

his kindness to us in Christ Jesus. [8] For it is by grace you have been saved, through faith—and this is not from yourselves, it is the gift of God— [9] not by works, so that no one can boast.

[10] For we are God's handiwork, created in Christ Jesus to do good works, which God prepared in advance for us to do."

Ephesians 2:1-10

You may be in a place in your life where you know you are "saved" because you have spoken out the words that go something like this:

Lord, I know that I am a sinner. I realize that there is nothing I can do under my own power to save myself from sin. I believe that you sent your son, Jesus, to pay the price for my sin. He died, was buried, and rose again to eternal life to save me from my sins. I ask Jesus to come into my heart right now, and to help me to turn away from every sin in my life, that I would be made a new creation.

If you have never prayed the sinner's prayer, I encourage you to pray it right now with all your heart. You can trust that God, who is faithful and merciful, not wishing that any should be separated from Him for eternity, will meet you right where you are and begin a beautiful work in your life – as you continue to surrender your life to Him day by day.

If you have been "saved" for quite some time, but are not experiencing "fruit" in your life as a believer and follower of Jesus, then you are right where I was 6 years ago. In God's kingdom, fruit is defined in Galatians 5:22-23:

"But the fruit of the Spirit is love, joy, peace, forbearance, kindness, goodness, faithfulness, [23] gentleness and self-control. Against such things there is no law."

By outward appearances, I had it all together and was blessed. By 2013, we had a really nice house in an affluent suburb, and were building a lake house. We had 3 cars and a nanny to help me as I worked as an engineering consultant. We lacked for nothing physically and rarely told our children no when they asked for the newest toy or game. We were building our own kingdom on this earth – doing what we thought we were supposed to be doing. Certainly, we were doing what the rest of the world around us was doing. Yet, at that time, despite having four kids who were full of hugs and laughter, I felt empty most of the time.

The impact of the trauma and neglect that I had experienced as a child did not magically go away as I grew up and became a parent myself. The hurt just got buried way down deep. There were so many times that I would be feeling an emotion like sorrow or anger, but have no idea where it was coming from. Literally, it was like the connection between my brain and my heart had been severed so that there was no two-way communication between the two. I could be talking on the phone to one of my sisters and they would ask me if I was ok because they could hear sadness in my voice. I would say that I was ok, but honestly, I didn't think I was. However, I could not figure out through my own intellect what was going on with me.

I wished I could say that I masked my hurt well, but my husband and kids would tell you differently. The truth is that my hurt came out as yelling, screaming, and shouting within our own house. I didn't know any other way to be heard. Remember that I had 4 children in 5 years. In amongst the diapers, the breast feeding, the house chores, and my job, there wasn't much time left for self-reflection or self-help. I knew the way I was coping with the stress and pressure of life wasn't working, but I didn't know what else to do.

We went to church every Sunday. I enjoyed the singing and the messages. I would often cry silently while in the service. There was nothing about church that gave me hope that my life could or should be different. I looked around and thought that everyone else must be doing better than I was. I thought there must have been something wrong with me that I could not feel real love, or that I was so often completely lacking patience, or that I seemed incapable of gentleness.

Lifted Up

In the fall of 2013, my father-in-law, Jerry, passed away. It was a cold October day. I remember it well. That morning on the way to work I had a minor car accident involving a semi that was barreling down on me on the interstate. Traffic ahead of me was slowing but the truck driver seemed to be accelerating as I looked into my rear-view mirror. To avoid getting squished, I swerved into the lane to my right and hit the side of an old pickup. The semi just kept going as he switched lanes to the left. I had to pull over to share my insurance information with the other driver in the pickup. The police came which took a while. I ended up being late for work.

(I had taken a long-term contracting assignment with a large insurance firm in town. I was responsible for leading a team of about 15 people for 3 months and was just in the middle of that work when my boss came in to the team room and asked for me to follow her.)

Of course, right away I got a pit in my stomach knowing that something was not right. I followed her into a small conference room nearby. She told me that my father in law had just passed away and that my mother in law needed me to meet her at the hospital where his body had been taken.

This was one of those days in my life that is forever etched in my mind, body, and heart. We all have these "special" days that we would like to be able to forget, but they invariably change us at the core.

It's interesting to think about "those days" that seem to change everything and stick with us. The first one of those that I can remember happened in elementary school. My class had been called to the Library resource room. There was a large TV in front of the class and we were being asked to be quiet. A man came onto the screen and told us that we were moments away from watching the Challenger Space Shuttle launch. You may also recall this event which became known as the Challenger Disaster. The space shuttle launched on January 28, 1986 and broke up 73 seconds into flight, killing all 7 astronauts on board which included the first teacher that was to go into space. As I reflect, this event may have been what sparked an interest in space travel for me, and caused me to sign up for Space Camp several years later!

Back to **October 24, 2013** – I ended up leaving work while holding back tears. I made it to my car and a great deluge of weeping commenced. Somehow, I was able to drive to the hospital and found my way to the room that Nancy was waiting in with Jerry's body. Her neighbor, Rose, was sitting with her as I came in. I won't ever forget seeing Jerry lying in that hospital bed with a sheet pulled up to his chest. It still looked like him, but the life force was no longer there in his body.

Garrick was out of town on that day, having flown out to Boston a couple days before to see his brother, Jeff, and Jeff's wife Denise. Both brothers are die-hard Red Sox fans. It was Game 1 of the World Series between the Red Sox and Cardinals being played in Boston. Boston had had a big victory the night before as they watched, and then celebrated together. It was early the next morning that Nancy called Jeff to tell him and Garrick that their father had passed away from a massive heart attack.

Dr. Gerald Duane Baxter, Ph.D. was a life-long educator holding seven degrees of his own. He knew how to teach and to reach young minds and had done so at both the college and secondary level. In the two years prior to Jerry's passing, God had placed a dream in my heart to start a Christian school in the area of the city we lived in, though I am not an educator myself, nor had ever even wanted to be a teacher. I had worked extremely hard in my own strength to try to make that school a reality, bringing local Lutheran school officials and Lutheran church leaders together. However, it was like God closed the door on that in September, the month before Jerry passed away.

It was on the day of Jerry's funeral that I first truly "experienced" God in an unmistakable way (as an adult). After Jerry's memorial service and reception, family members had come back to our house. I felt the need to be alone, so I had gone upstairs to our bedroom. I was kneeling on the floor next to our bed, with my Bible open in front of me, crying out to God in my sorrow for the loss of Jerry, but also in my desperation for feeling like I had failed God, having been unable to get a new Christian school up off the ground.

I needed to hear from God and the only way I thought that He communicated was through His Word. Surely, I would find comfort in the words of the Bible. It was then, in that moment, that I heard God speak to me for the first time. I did not hear an audible voice, but I distinctly heard God speak from the inside of me. He told me to "call Heidi". I knew who He was referring to, but I didn't know why I would call her at that time. She was an acquaintance of mine but not really someone I would call a friend. I had met her through MOPS (mothers of preschoolers).

I am surprised at my obedience now that I would call her. I'm surprised because, at that time, I was very guarded and would rarely allow someone else to see me in a vulnerable state. I was prideful and believed that I had to always be strong and have all the answers. To need someone else and to ask for help meant that I couldn't do something on my own, which I thought meant that I wasn't capable. Of course, I now know this way of thinking is a lie, but at that time, self-dependence was all I was conditioned to understand.

So, I called Heidi—and she answered. I uncomfortably told her that I didn't know why I was really calling her, but I felt like maybe God had prompted me to do so, if that were possible. She was so encouraging to me. She listened intently and then immediately shared a story from a ministry that she was a part of called A Lighted Path, which operates in Malawi, Africa. She told me that they were looking for a location for a community center there. People met here in Omaha, while another group of people met in Malawi. Together they prayed and listened for God to tell them where to go. She called this a "Pray and Seek".

This sounded a bit crazy to me at first, but then she told me that the Lord led them to a specific building quite miraculously that was the perfect location for a community center. This building used to house another missionary group that provided meals to the community, but it had shut down just a week before. A Lighted Path was planning to provide meals to the community as a part of their mission. This building just so happened to be the PERFECT location, because it came complete with everything needed to provide the meals, including people to serve the meal. It was like God knew that this other ministry would close and so he sent A Lighted Path there to meet the need! Could it be that God knows what will happen before it does?! Well, yes, of course. God is not on our timeline. Recall from Isaiah 46:10 that the Lord wrote the end from the beginning!

Heidi suggested that we do a "Pray and Seek" for the Christian school I had been working so hard to make happen. At that point, I felt like I had nothing left to lose so I figured why not. She offered to help me put a small group together so that we could do this *little experiment.*

It happened a couple of weeks later, but I was not able to participate because one of my kids went into Children's Hospital with croup. While a few people met at our church, including our Senior Pastor Keith, another group left in a car. The people at the church prayed and listened for what the Lord was saying, either directly through His Word (as He would send them to various scriptures), or according to the pictures He would give to them in their mind's eye. These messages were relayed via cell phone text to the people in the car who drove the route as they felt led by God to do so.

In the next chapter, I will share with you the result of that "Pray and Seek" and what God has done since that time to help me lay down my own dreams, so that I can receive His. I can tell you this... since that day in October 2013, when I first experienced God through the power of Holy Spirit in a tangible way, nothing in my life is the same as it was before. And I am so thankful, because His plans for me (and you) are truly better than anything we could plan for ourselves.

A few months later in January of 2014, a friend of mine, Kari, who I was in a small ladies' church group with, was sharing with us how she had been going through something called "Whole Heart". She explained to us that she would meet with a guy named Pastor Chuck and another lady named Kathy once a week for a couple of hours—and it was totally free. That was a bit of a red flag to me, because I was smart enough to know that "nothing is free". I had spent thousands of dollars and hundreds of hours on counseling with therapists over my lifetime to that point, so I knew that it cost something, even for people to help you.

She said that they were helping her to work through hurts from a long time ago, and even new hurts that had come through marriage and parenting. I was surprised to hear that she had hurts. She seemed to have everything all together. Isn't it interesting how we make those snap judgments about people's lives without really knowing? I just assumed that her life was perfect, because it looked like on the surface that she had a good marriage and well-mannered children. What a lie! The truth is that there isn't a person living on this earth who hasn't been hurt in some way. And without healing at the core, the impact of a hurt can go on long after even the memory of it.

I was intrigued by this thing she called *Whole Heart*. If Kari needed help, though her life and history seemed pretty good on the surface, then I must have needed a whole lot of help! I knew I wasn't free of my past. My life seemed pretty unmanageable most days. I was working so hard to try to hold everything in my life together; the word "striving" is a word I knew so well. I would strive under my own strength to perform at work so that I would be considered valuable to my client. I would strive as a wife to meet the needs of my husband, though so often any interaction with him would turn into an argument, as both of us vied for power in our relationship. As a mother, I was so incredibly busy just feeding, bathing, dressing, and hauling my kids around that showing affection to them was an afterthought or no thought at all.

I remember the moment that I called Pastor Chuck. I was on my lunch break at work and I got up the courage to call him to make an appointment. I was standing in a large lower level lobby area near the escalators. I felt like anyone who passed me must have known I was making a call for help because I couldn't do it on my own anymore. The phone rang and rang and it went to voicemail. I was relieved to not have to *get into it* with Pastor Chuck. I left my name and number and he called back later that day. We set a time to meet and I checked that task off my list.

I was so nervous on the evening of my first session, but at the same time, I was really hopeful that this guy was going to be able to really help me. I felt like I needed to be able to perform at a high level all the time, but I was letting myself and my family down every day. Maybe now, Pastor Chuck would "fix me" once and for all so that I could be what everyone else needed me to be.

Boy was I disappointed when some of the first words out of Chuck's mouth were that he wasn't going to help me! What? Had I heard incorrectly? He went on to say that he and Kathy were there to pray with me and for me, but it would be me that would talk to God and ask Him to come into my heart to provide the healing that I needed.

Hmmm... to say I was skeptical was an understatement. Besides feeling led by God to call Heidi that one time, and feeling led to various scriptures, I had not "interacted" with God as they were suggesting I would do. I didn't know how to talk to God and I certainly didn't know how to *hear* from God. I believed that God could bring healing, but if he wanted to heal me in some crazy way, wouldn't He have already done that?

Chuck explained to me the process very briefly: he told me that from the time I was in my mother's womb until today, I have been hurt by people, circumstances, and events. I didn't know how to ask God to be my protector as a young child, so I tried to protect myself. With each hurt that came in, a little crack would appear in my heart. With each big hurt, pieces of my heart would even break off, disconnecting from the other parts. Because my heart wasn't whole as God intended it to be, and I had all these protectors at work (anger, shame, guilt, etc.) in me, I wasn't able to fully be who God intended me to be.

This really resonated with me. I knew that the ways I was trying to cope were not working. I also knew that I carried resentments and unforgiveness in my heart for things that people had done to me. I tried my best to be okay, but if I was being honest with myself, I was merely surviving and not thriving.

Chuck said that He would invite Holy Spirit in (to our meeting I guessed) and then he would ask me some questions, which I would sometimes be told to repeat after him, and then I would speak out the first thing that came to my mind.

Question number 1:
Do I trust God to protect me in all circumstances? *Um, no. Is He supposed to?*

Question number 2:
Do I trust God to provide for me in all circumstances? *No, again.*

Didn't I go hungry many times as a child because my mom was too busy drinking and my dad was nowhere to be found? Wasn't it my job to provide for myself? Hadn't I worked hard from the time I was old enough to get a job to earn money, so that I would always have food and the things that I needed for myself?

The next six to eight weeks were some of the hardest in my life, as Chuck facilitated the process of allowing Holy Spirit to come into my heart and shine a light on the dark places that had developed. All the layers of protection I had built around my own heart began to come down. Like an onion being peeled back layer by layer, a pungent aroma was released that caused burning and tears!

With each session, a new hidden memory of the first time I experienced fear, or the first time I experienced shame, would come forward. It hurt to remember these things, but something began to take place *after* the memory was released.

For the first time in my life, I felt God's presence *come into* each situation. It's like He was there when it happened, and instead of my carrying the burden, He took it. It's not easy to explain the sensation that was both physical and spiritual, but I felt a warmth come into my body and my spirit. It was like dark heavy chunks were removed and I became lighter somehow.

I began to see pictures very clearly of moments in time from the womb, through my toddler years, teen years, and into my adult years. The first time I experienced hunger was shown to be when I was only days old, lying on a changing table. I was so hungry and so I cried and cried, but no one came to feed me. This was the first time I found my thumb on my right hand and began sucking it for comfort. Interestingly, my thumb sucking continued until I was more than ten years old. When I became old enough that I was embarrassed about doing it in front of others, I stopped myself. But I would still do it as I slept at night.

We tried putting a sock on my hand when I went to bed, but I would always find that in the morning I had taken it off and my thumb was soggy. So then, we took the next step of taping the sock onto my arm, which ended up giving me a rash. Eventually, I think it was mind over matter that prevailed. Unfortunately, the harm of thumb sucking had been done as my teeth will testify. There is a gap on the right side of my teeth where the thumb used to fit!

Other memories weren't so easy to understand or commonplace as feeling hunger. In one experience in dealing with the need to control, as God's presence *came into* the situation, I literally felt something *come out* of me. As it was coming out, it caused me to cry out and groan in agony. My body posture changed from a relaxed state, sitting on the couch, to standing up with my back arched unnaturally as I seemed to cough something out. After it was over, I opened my eyes expecting Chuck and Kathy to be surprised or alarmed, but both looked just as calm as ever. Apparently what had just happened was a common occurrence for them! I was relieved to not be any crazier than others! They did not tell me, but I know now that this was what deliverance sometimes looked like.

Lifted Up

Week by week, God did begin to heal my heart from the inside out. Memory by memory, hurt by hurt, root by root, God's presence came in as I was able to work through forgiveness and repentance. I learned that forgiveness is the key to it all! Any why should that be a surprise to us? Doesn't the Bible tell us that we are to ask forgiveness and also forgive those that trespass against us?

> *"If we confess our sins, he is faithful and just and will forgive us our sin sand purify us from all unrighteousness."* 1 John 1:9

> *"For if you forgive other people when they sin against you, your heavenly Father will also forgive you. [15] But if you do not forgive others their sins, your Father will not forgive your sins."*
> *Matthew 6:14-15*

To be honest, I did not realize how much unforgiveness I was carrying in my heart. I knew that I had experienced a lot of tough stuff in my life, but who doesn't? Wasn't I just supposed to move on? The people who hurt me just did the best they could, right?

Here is the truth that I have come to know which I believe is wisdom from God Himself: God's heart for you and for me is that we would never suffer for any reason.

However, the keys to the kingdom of this world were handed over from Adam to Satan when Eve and Adam ate the fruit. Because of this, sin entered into the world. Because God will never force Himself on any-one, a person may choose to sin, and this causes hurt to another person. Each of us has a choice to make as we move through life moment by moment to follow God's will for our lives, to forgive as we need to, and to ask forgiveness when we lose our way. As we follow His will, He guides us and protects us. Here is the way David speaks of this protection that can only be found in the Lord:

My Whole Hearted Testimony

If you say, "The LORD is my refuge,"
and you make the Most High your dwelling,
[10] no harm will overtake you,
no disaster will come near your tent.
[11] For he will command his angels concerning you
to guard you in all your ways;
[12] they will lift you up in their hands,
so that you will not strike your foot against a stone.
[13] You will tread on the lion and the cobra;
you will trample the great lion and the serpent.

"Because he loves me," says the LORD, "I will rescue him;
I will protect him, for he acknowledges my name.
[15] He will call on me, and I will answer him;
I will be with him in trouble,
I will deliver him and honor him.
[16] With long life I will satisfy him
and show him my salvation."
Psalms 91:9-16

If we live outside of His will, our lives quickly become unmanageable. A hurt comes in, I get mad, and I start telling myself a story about the person who hurt me. This leads to judgment and resentment. Instead of giving my hurt to the Lord right away, choosing to forgive the other person, a little crack that I cannot see but is surely there appears in my heart. If that hurt is not dealt with, a root of unforgiveness grows.

God's intention for each of us is that we would never know a time apart from him, where we trust Him to provide and protect us in all situations.

It is certainly His heart for children that they would be taught this truth from the earliest age. Unfortunately, this is not what the world teaches today. And, why should it since this world is under the power of Satan whose deepest desire is to see each child of God suffer in this life and die a death eternally apart from God.

Lifted Up

It is these roots of unforgiveness that separate us from God and create a legal right for the enemy, Satan, to come against us. If my heart is whole, meaning there is no unforgiveness or unrepentance present, then there is nothing separating me from God. What I learned as I went through the Whole Heart process is that God created me (and you) with the ability to hear His voice. But when sin comes in and is not dealt with, a barrier comes between me and Him. Satan can then use this barrier to gain access to us.

You may not realize this, but you are able to hear three voices in your mind: your own, God's voice, or Satan's. Your heart is like a tuning fork and depending on the state of your heart, you can be tuned in to a voice that you do not want to be hearing.

Have you ever wondered why psychics are able to know things about you? First of all, you need to realize that they are operating in witch-craft, which God is not okay with.

> "'Do not turn to mediums or seek out spiritists, for you will be
> defiled by them. I am the Lord your God."   Leviticus 19:31

So psychics are either just making things up or they are actually tuning into the spiritual world, which is made up of both good and evil. We need to recognize that there is a whole world going on around us that we do not see with our eyes. And just because we do not see it, does not mean that it is not just as real as the physical world.

As my heart became pure before the Lord, I began to receive pictures that did not come up from my imagination, but instead came up from my Spirit, which is connected to Holy Spirit. If I am living in sin, then I could just as easily receive pictures or words from Satan and his camp of demons. Obviously I do not want to receive messages from Satan, so what can I do? Well, after my Whole Heart sessions were completed (I guess you could say I graduated), I was instructed on how to continue to walk out forgiveness and repentance on my own, and how to determine if my heart was remaining whole.

This is critical to understand. You may have received "inner healing" at some point in your life, and have been frustrated by the lack of "fruit" in your life following the healing. God is absolutely capable of fully and completely healing our wounds, but it is up to us to continue to ask Him in to help us break patterns of behavior that cause us to receive new hurts.

A wonderful lady named Lisa Max (who leads a ministry called Let the Children Fly) taught me this lesson: Satan only has three weapons he can use against us: they are 1) hurts, 2) lies, and 3) offenses. Any time we experience a hurt, we believe a lie, or we become offended, we give Satan a legal right to enter into our heart and mind to do further damage. Any time we choose to take a hurt to the Father to be forgiven, we take back that legal right. Any time we choose to rebuke a lie in the name of Jesus, we take back the legal right. Any time we choose to NOT become offended by something someone does, or we choose to forgive someone of the offense right away, we take back the legal right from the enemy of our souls. It is as easy as this:

**Abba, Father - I choose to forgive (_____) for doing (_____).
I place my hurt under the cross covered in Jesus blood, fully forgiven and severed from my life. I choose to bless (_____) and ask you to bless them. I ask forgiveness for my sin of unforgiveness for (_____) and place my sin under the cross completely covered in Jesus blood and fully forgiven.**

I then ask myself this question, **"Is it okay if the Lord would come close to you?"** and I let my heart speak the YES back to the Lord. Then I ask in a different way, **"Is it okay if the Lord would take you all the way into His heart?"** and again my heart says yes and I wait for His presence to come, which it always does because He is so good and His love for me is without end.

Not too hard, right? Well, actually, at first it can be very challenging to recognize when a hurt has come in that needs forgiveness. A tell-tale sign that I need to forgive someone for something may look like me replaying an interaction between them in my head, and trying to think of different responses I should have given them to show them their fault. Or perhaps I am replaying a situation over and over in my head and pointing out all the ways that they have wronged me. Any time we have a one-way negative dialogue going in our head, we can be alerted that a door has been opened and the voice we are hearing is either our own or Satan's.

Satan loves to be our accuser, but fortunately we have someone, Jesus, who intercedes for us.

Then I heard a loud voice in heaven say:

"Now have come the salvation and the power
and the kingdom of our God,
and the authority of his Messiah.
For the accuser of our brothers and sisters,
who accuses them before our God day and night,
has been hurled down.

Revelation 12:10

I believe we are living in a time where God is making available to us new tools, or perhaps ancient tools made available again, so that we can learn to live with clean hearts which enable clear thinking and seeing.

As I went through Whole Heart, my heart was healed from deep wounds. I then learned how to live each day so that new wounds could not take hold. I began to hear and see from God's perspective more and more as my heart was tuned to Him, and not tuned to the enemy or the ways of the world. This is an ongoing process that I believe we are to continue to work out with the Lord.

August 26th, 2015 – A word from the Lord

"Rachel, dear daughter of the one true God. You are beginning to see the plan I have laid out since before the beginning of time. My plan for relationship and my plan for redemption. You have been chosen to live at this time in this age of the ultimate reformation. My body will come into unity like never before under the power and authority of my Son as head of the body. It will be He that leads the great army into victory over the fallen one. He will allow his countenance to fall upon those people, my children, who have given themselves over fully and completely, with all abandonment of flesh, for them to not only be remade in His image, but to walk in His full power and authority over every realm of darkness.

I have spoken of this to you before, but only now do you appreciate the gravity of the words I've given to you. This is not about you, sweet girl. This is about My plan. Fear not that you have somehow disappointed me. You've lived your life well. Now that you have come into this season of wholeness of heart, you can finally see what you have been created for.

Worry not, for you do carry an ample measure of humility. I know your heart, daughter, and you are worthy of the mantle I give you to carry. The assignment is not beyond you, for I will equip you. The testing and trials have not ended but I will also give you joy throughout. The joy in all circumstances is yours to claim. You are a part of the Order of Melchizedek, not through your own might, for you could not earn this distinction. I call you into the greatest service to me. It is a service of great cost. The cost is everything and all that you are. The cost will be greater than you can pay on your own, but I will make up the difference. You were not born for this life, but to experience the fullness of the life eternal. All that you've experienced the last thirty-eight years of your life is nothing compared to the heavenly home I've prepared for you. I will show you."

Stepping into Healing

As a starting place, ask the Lord to show you the areas of your life that continue to be impacted by deep hurts you've experienced. Is there an active root to hurt in your life that is keeping you from the plans God has for you? You might even want to make a list of people who have hurt you and what they did to hurt.

This is not an activity in "keeping a list of wrongs" because the Lord instructs us that we are not to do that. After you have made the list, then enter in to prayer with the Lord. Ask the Holy Spirit to come in. It is only through God's power and presence that these words can actually bring change and healing. Recite the prayer below over and over again until you have declared forgiveness and repentance for these things.

Abba, Father – I choose to forgive ___(who)___ for ____(what)_____.

I place my hurt under the cross covered in Jesus blood, fully forgiven and severed from my life. I choose to bless ___(who)__ and ask you to bless them.

I ask forgiveness for my sin of unforgiveness towards __(who)__ and place my sin under the cross, completely covered in Jesus blood and fully forgiven.

Then ask yourself this question, "**Is it okay if Jesus would come close to you?**" and let your heart speak the YES back to the Lord.

Then ask in a different way, "**Is it okay if the Lord would take you all the way into His heart?**" and again let your heart says yes and wait for His presence to come, which it always does because He is so good and His love for you is without end.

Does that mean you are fully healed? Maybe not, but our words do carry power, and it is a great first step towards bringing reconciliation into your life, setting you free from the hurt you are carrying.

My Whole Hearted Testimony

The One Whole Heart ministry, birthed through Pastor Chuck DeVetter, is headquartered in Omaha, Nebraska. A network of facilitators to the Whole Heart process has been established. You can receive this inner healing remotely and without charge. For more information, please see the website: www.onewholeheartministry.com

CHAPTER 5: Be Who I Created You To Be

While going through Whole Heart, Chuck would always end the sessions by praying over me. He and Kathy would have me stand and they would stand next to me. Kathy would commonly put her hand on my back and Chuck would sometimes place one of his fingers against my forehead. This *kind* of praying was new to me! As a Lutheran, I was taught to fold my hands and close my eyes. If I prayed, I was to do it quietly to myself. Of course, I would often say "Oh, I will pray for you" if I heard that someone was hurting or if had lost a loved one, but I never stopped to do it right there; and to be honest, usually I would forget the commitment a minute after I made it.

This experience of receiving prayer was different. Chuck and Kathy actually prayed for me right there. They spoke words of encouragement over me. In another first for me, Chuck would pray in this "new" voice I did not understand. I could feel peace in the environment which I had come to expect in Holy Spirit's presence. I knew that Chuck was praying to Father God and Jesus. But what was this sound coming out of his lips?

Well, I learned that it was called "tongues". After a few sessions ending with this type of prayer, Chuck asked me if I wanted to be able to pray in tongues. I thought, why not? So, I nodded and he gave me some simple instructions. He told me that I was to just open my mouth and begin making the sounds he was making as he prayed in tongues. He began to speak and sounds began to come forth from me too. In my head, I was literally thinking to myself, "I love you, Jesus," but what came out as I opened my mouth was a strange but pleasing sound! Literally, I felt this stirring inside my chest right where my breast bones come together. This sensation started there and then proceeded to come up out of my chest into my throat and out of my lips! I felt like it was truly miraculous!

Chuck encouraged me to practice this gift so that I would grow in confidence in using it with the Lord alone, and when it was appropriate in groups as we "prayed in the Spirit". I would practice in my car where no one would know that I was doing this *odd* thing to my God. The more that I practiced, the more that my prayer language expanded. As of today, I feel like it is still just a handful of syllables, but it suffices.

What is the point of a prayer language you might ask? Well, the biggest thing for me is that when I don't know what to pray, I can always be assured that when I pray in my prayer language to God, He hears it and He understands. It is always the perfect prayer because it is from Him to Him.

I distinctly recall the first time I admitted speaking in tongues to my mom. She was more than skeptical, which is her nature. Lutherans do not believe in speaking in tongues. Actually, I think Lutherans believe the *Gifts of the Spirit* are no longer available.

> *"Now about the gifts of the Spirit, brothers and sisters, I do not want you to be uninformed. [2] You know that when you were pagans, somehow or other you were influenced and led astray to mute idols. [3] Therefore I want you to know that no one who is speaking by the Spirit of God says, "Jesus be cursed," and no one can say, "Jesus is Lord," except by the Holy Spirit.*
>
> *[4] There are different kinds of gifts, but the same Spirit distributes them. [5] There are different kinds of service, but the same Lord. [6] There are different kinds of working, but in all of them and in everyone it is the same God at work.*
>
> *7 Now to each one the manifestation of the Spirit is given for the common good. 8 To one there is given through the Spirit a message of wisdom, to another a message of knowledge by means of the same Spirit, 9 to another faith by the same Spirit, to another gifts of healing by that one Spirit,*

10 to another miraculous powers, to another prophecy, to another distinguishing between spirits, to another speaking in different kinds of tongues, and to still another the interpretation of tongues.

All these are the work of one and the same Spirit, and he distributes them to each one, just as he determines."

1 Corinthians 12:1-11

My mom and I had gone outside to sit and enjoy a lovely warm summer evening. We sat together at the picnic table under the patio umbrella. I offered to speak my prayer language so that she could hear it because she seemed interested. So I did... and her eyes got a little big and she seemed surprised. It was hard to argue against the reality that it was a language not of my own.

If you have never heard someone speak in tongues, I can tell you that each person that I have heard truly sounds different. I've never heard two people sound exactly alike, though I know that some people speak in actual foreign languages as the Apostle Luke describes beginning in the Book of Acts, chapter 2:

> *"When the day of Pentecost came, they were all together in one place. [2] Suddenly a sound like the blowing of a violent wind came from heaven and filled the whole house where they were sitting. [3] They saw what seemed to be tongues of fire that separated and came to rest on each of them. [4] All of them were filled with the Holy Spirit and began to speak in other tongues as the Spirit enabled them.*
>
> *[5] Now there were staying in Jerusalem God-fearing Jews from every nation under heaven. [6] When they heard this sound, a crowd came together in bewilderment, because each one heard their own language being spoken. [7] Utterly amazed, they asked: "Aren't all these who are speaking Galileans?*

My Whole Hearted Testimony

[8] Then how is it that each of us hears them in our native language? [9] Parthians, Medes and Elamites; residents of Mesopotamia, Judea and Cappadocia, Pontus and Asia, [10] Phrygia and Pamphylia, Egypt and the parts of Libya near Cyrene; visitors from Rome [11] (both Jews and converts to Judaism); Cretans and Arabs—we hear them declaring the wonders of God in our own tongues!" [12] Amazed and perplexed, they asked one another, "What does this mean?"

Acts 2:1-12

I had the privilege of hearing a wonderful testimony concerning someone speaking in tongues in a foreign language to someone else without knowing that that was what they were doing. A couple of years back in a very large local Lutheran Church in Omaha called King of Kings, a woman prayed over a traveling pastor, who had stepped into the prayer room and then received a distressing phone call. After the pastor completed the call, this lady offered to pray for him. Without knowing it, she prayed in her prayer language; unbeknownst to her, she spoke to him in perfect Hebrew.

Later that day, this pastor had supper with another couple, a pastor and his wife, Krista. He relayed to the couple what had happened in the prayer room earlier in the day and how surprised he was that someone from this Omaha church knew Hebrew. He had gone on to thank her in Hebrew assuming she could understand and told her the name God had given her in Hebrew, as he felt God had directed him to do.

Sometime later, the story came full circle. Another friend of mine, Heidi (the one who I called on the day of my father-in-law's funeral and who directed us to pray-and-seek), was ministering to a lady named Kim through Whole Heart. Kim, a member of King of Kings, ended up sharing a story of praying in tongues over a traveling pastor who had stepped into their prayer room. Upon hearing Kim mention this, Heidi, who had heard the other side of the story from Krista, who met with this Pastor that same night, was then able to encourage Kim with what God had done through her prayer language.

Lifted Up

It turned out that Kim, without knowing it, had prayed in tongues over this pastor, and she had done so using perfect Hebrew, which this pastor knew fluently. Kim was stunned. She was excited to know that God had used her in this special way, but also disappointed because she had been asking God to reveal to her what her heavenly name was. Upon finding out that this pastor did share her new name, she was bummed to think that he had given it to her wrongly assuming she knew Hebrew!

The syllables in my prayer language seem to change somewhat with the season I am in. There is one phrase that I began to hear over and over again. It sounds like this phonetically, "Sell-o-kay-see-oh-ko-so-shay". I asked the Lord about it in one special encounter and He said that it meant, "I am yours and you are mine." That sounded pretty good to me. Sometime later I found the scriptural reference to this from Song of Songs 6:3a,

"I am my beloved's and my beloved is mine"

Speaking in tongues was a pretty minor change compared to the other changes that began to take place in me. As my heart was healed, I began to really trust God to be my *protector* in all circumstances. I began to trust God to *provide* for me in all circumstances. This sounds like a really good thing, right? Well, it really is a great thing for a person to truly believe this. But the reality is that I still lived in a very broken world, surrounded by people who had not been fully healed themselves. The people closest to me didn't understand or agree with my newfound "truth" and "freedom" in the Lord.

Though I could see the fruit for myself—being able to put others before myself, not needing to control every situation, not desiring to manipulate others around me anymore—it felt like the positive changes didn't seem to account for much with the people I loved.

The truth is, the next five years were the hardest of my life, though they have were also the best in so many ways. It's hard for me to even write about this but I know that I must. The tale I have to tell is one of God's greatest gifts of mercy being poured out abundantly. The most recent years of my life have been polar-opposite to any other period. My story is one of death and new life, and so I will persevere to tell it. Even today as I write this, it is the changes in me and my viewpoint that cause a wide chasm between me and my closest loved ones, and between the world around me and where I am. I am becoming who God made me to be, and this transformation is not without trials and pain. Though my faith remains through it all that God will fulfill His promise to complete this good work He began in me.

> *"Being confident of this, that he who began a good work in you will carry it on to completion until the day of Christ Jesus."*
> *Philippians 1:6*

Would I have done what I believe God called me to do if I would have known how hard it would be? Of course, because I love God—there is nothing I would not do for Him. There is nothing I will withhold from Him. However, I really had no idea how hard things would be for me. I guess I had this misconception that when you are working for God's kingdom, doors just open for you.

I wrongly assumed that others would see God's hand at work and just jump on-board. When I looked at other people who had stepped out to advance God's kingdom, I must have missed the challenges they faced. I didn't see the persecution that comes with it. I also didn't recognize how much flesh of my own I still carried, that God would need to burn away. Death to self is painful. I can see that now, but when I became spirit-filled in October 2013, I didn't know what I was in for. You see, God is jealous for our heart. He wants all of it. He made us a perfect creation, but in this world that belongs to Satan right now, we don't operate as a perfect creation.

Lifted Up

Call to Action:

Do you know if you are Spirit-Filled? If the answer is no, you can ask the Lord to become filled by His spirit. Do it now. Just pray…

Father God, I love you. I'm not satisfied with my current relationship with you. I want more of you and I am willing to give you more of me. I ask you, Holy Spirit, to come into my heart and my mind and my life. I ask you to touch me so that I can feel you. I ask you to pour yourself out into me, a willing vessel. Fill me Lord so that I am changed.

You can also ask someone who you know is Spirit-Filled to lay hands on you and pray for you to be filled with the Spirit, just as the disciples did in the first days after Pentecost.

My Whole Hearted Testimony

CHAPTER 6: Pray, Listen and Have Faith

Now I must tell you the story of Valor. In a previous chapter, I told you that I felt Holy Spirit direct me to call Heidi, and when I did she suggested we do a pray-and-seek to find a school site for the school that I was trying to launch in the part of the city we lived in at the time. Well, the people who participated in that adventure were led south of Omaha along Highway 370. They turned down a gravel road off the highway and kept heading south with corn fields and bean fields as far as the eye could see... Until, out of the clear blue, they spotted buildings perched on a hill towards the west. They kept driving and ended up pulling into the paved driveway of Nebraska Christian College. Those in the car had not ever been out that way and were completed surprised to see a college—just off a gravel road!

On **November 8th, 2013** Garrick and I met with Dave Miller, head of their Marketing department at NCC. I really didn't know what to expect. I wasn't sure how to share how we had been supernaturally led to their location. I knew Dave would likely think I was crazy. Dave gave us a tour of the various buildings and helped us to better understand the purpose of the college, to equip church workers.

I asked Dave if he thought there was room on the campus to house a small primary school. He said, "We don't have any space, but we've got land." It turned out they were looking to improve their cash and debt situation and were considering the sale of around forty acres adjacent to the campus. At the end of the tour, we met in a large, open room with windows facing the gravel road. As we were talking, a big yellow school bus pulled onto the property at the main entrance and parked. Dave remarked, "Well, I've never seen that before." We smiled at each other and wondered if that was a sign from God about what He wanted to do. The last significant thing that came from this meeting was that Dave was telling us about a school they recruited from for their enrollment. It was a school in Colorado named Valor which he spoke highly of.

After the meeting, I didn't clearly know what next steps to take. We had a number of volunteers who were helping with planning who were excited at the progress. We decided to pray over the land and continue to seek the Lord. I walked the land several times praying and asking the Lord what He intended, though I didn't receive an answer.

Nebraska Christian offered to sell the land for one million dollars. It might as well have been 100 million because I had no idea how to raise money. It seemed like a dead-end, at least for that season. To this day, I don't know why the Lord first led us there, though I trust that He did. Perhaps it was only to give us the name Valor, because after that, we began to refer to the dream I carried in my heart to start a school as *Valor*.

The Lord showed me that the name would be perfectly fitting to what He wanted to create in the years ahead. You see, Gideon was called the mighty man of Valor by an angel of God who had been sent to him. Gideon was from the lowliest of tribes and was the little squirt brother.

There was nothing mighty about him—but with the Lord, he was about to do miraculous things and it would be all to God's glory, not his own. It was the same with our school Valor. The children from all different walks of life may look weak and scrawny, but through God, they WILL do mighty things to advance His kingdom, which is coming to the earth!

On **November 12th, 2013** I prayed and felt the Lord direct me to 2 Kings 12:9

> *"Jehoiada the priest took a chest and bored a hole in its lid. He placed it beside the altar, on the right side as one enters the temple of the Lord. The priests who guarded the entrance put into the chest all the money that was brought to the temple of the Lord."*

My Whole Hearted Testimony

My comment in my journal was this:

> "The awareness that God will provide funds at just the right time. It could be as simple as taking a box and drilling a hole in its lid and placing it beside God's alter."

I seriously have to laugh upon reading this now. Hindsight is 20/20 as they say! I was such a babe in Christ. Because I didn't understand the ways of God (not that I fully do today, but I have grown), I naively thought that since God led us to this land, He was just going to provide the money. Period. He would show us what we needed to do, or He would just do the work and we would have all that we needed to start the school, as we understood it. Let me just tell you that I was wildly mistaken in that assumption. I learned the hard way that my ways are not His ways, and my timing is not His timing.

On my journey with the Lord, I've learned as much about myself as about Him. **I've learned that the greatest gift He gave me was the gift of faith.** (Recall this is one of the gifts of the Spirit from 2 Corinthians 12:9.)

I have a child-like faith that allows me to believe God for ANYTHING. If the *spirit cat* didn't surprise me, what would? God could rain diamonds from heaven today. He could, but He probably won't. Why not? He would only do it if it's part of His perfect plan and will. If it was the best thing for me, He would not withhold even diamonds. But only God knows what is really best for each of us.

Remember how I prayed and asked Him to let me *SEE* something in the spirit, but instead He chose to let me FEEL and HEAR the spirit cat instead. He knows what is best and **I do not**. But I trust Him for His best all the time. When I am frustrated with His timing, I have to remind myself that He knows what He is doing and I do not. The best any of us can hope for is to see a part of the big beautiful tapestry that is our life, being woven by the master craftsman.

Lifted Up

"For we know in part, and we prophesy in part."

1 Corinthians 13:9

Near the end of November of that year, I met with a lovely woman of God, Terri Lynn, who was the principal of the Christian school we had enrolled Zander in after a short stint in public school that proved a poor fit with our family and belief system. Terri Lynn was surprised to hear of the dream I harbored of starting a Christian school. She was very encouraging. I remember fondly her Bible sitting open on the middle of her desk, well-worn from use. She immediately turned to this scripture:

> *"For who hath despised the day of small things? for they shall rejoice, and shall see the plummet in the hand of Zerubbabel with those seven; they are the eyes of the Lord, which run to and fro through the whole earth."*   *Zechariah 4:10 KJV*

Well, we were definitely small, so that fit! Terri Lynn offered this additional word of wisdom which I do believe to be true. She said, "If it is God's vision, it will be His provision." At that point in my life, I was still not in the habit of self-reflection. Had I been, I would have asked a key question of myself: was I sure that this dream of starting a Christian school in Southwest Omaha was God's vision?

I did not ask that question, and so I went on assuming that this monumental task, as I understood it, was from Him. I was willing to strive under my own strength to make it happen one way or another. God had already closed the door on the school being a Lutheran school under the existing Lutheran school system that operated in the Omaha area. This had happened just weeks before Jerry's death, and led me to cry out to the Lord for guidance after his funeral.

In that conversation with Terri Lynn, she mentioned a Presbyterian church not far from my home in SW Omaha, that her school had at one time looked at for partnership of facilities. It turned out that for their school, it wasn't big enough; but she gave me the name of the church and suggested I pray about it. I left her office, looked up the number to the church, and called it. Do you notice which step I missed?

Prayer... shucks. I set a meeting with the pastor, and before I knew it I was sitting in front of him, sharing my vision for the school. He gave me a tour of the building and I could just see how perfect it would be. They even had a full-sized gym that would be perfect for events and weekly P.E. class.

By this time, we had a pretty sizable planning committee that was meeting regularly to choose curriculum, set schedules, and begin to document what we would offer and to whom. I met this church's board and we began scoping out the physical changes that would be needed to accommodate the school. This was my first introduction to the complex and difficult world of city and state regulations for the school environment. The most critical requirement that I came across was the hallway width of 6'. This church would need just minor changes to accommodate that.

At this same time, I was beginning to navigate the world of non-profit start-ups. I learned the term "501c3" intimately well. (If you are fortunate enough to have never come across that lingo, it refers to not-for-profit status granted by the Federal government.) I can look back now and see how God brought just the right people into my life at just the right time. In my research, I connected with another principal of a Christian school operating in Lincoln, Nebraska. He gave me the name of a Christian lawyer named Tom who was a partner at Baird Holm, a prestigious law firm in Omaha. Tom was able to steer me in the right direction to prepare a federal filing. I tried to do as much work as I could on my own, since Tom's law firm was not inexpensive to hire.

At this time, if felt like some doors would open and some doors would remain closed. I presented to my own church leadership team this dream to start a school. Unfortunately, the vision did not resonate with them. Our church already supported the local Lutheran school. They couldn't see why they would want to support a non-Lutheran school.

Lifted Up

My journal of this period of time is full of encouragement from the Lord. While I did not know His heart fully for this work I had embarked on, He was behind me in taking the steps of faith to bring it to fruition. I would pray while I was at work. I felt like I had to do it "undercover" because I thought if I was *caught* praying surely I would get in trouble somehow. I would do my "high-powered" engineering efficiency consulting work, leading teams of people, and then I would retreat to my desk for an hour to speak to the Lord and to ask Him to help me. These are some of the scriptures He sent me to during those times to help me continue to move forward:

"Here is my servant, whom I uphold,
my chosen one in whom I delight;
I will put my Spirit on him,
and he will bring justice to the nations.
² He will not shout or cry out,
or raise his voice in the streets.
³ A bruised reed he will not break,
and a smoldering wick he will not snuff out.
In faithfulness he will bring forth justice;
⁴ he will not falter or be discouraged
till he establishes justice on earth.
In his teaching the islands will put their hope."
Isaiah *42:1-4*

I felt like I was God's servant, really for the first time in my life. I was doing something for Him, something that I believed He had asked me to do.

Then I heard the voice of the Lord saying, "Whom shall I
send? And who will go for us?" And I said, "Here am I. Send me!"
Isaiah 6:8

In December of 2013, our youngest son Knox came down with a strange illness. He had a fever for several days, and the whites of his eyes turned blood red. We noticed a rash that started on his torso and eventually covered his whole body. I made an appointment with the doctor's office; we were not able to be seen by our assigned family doctor but they got us in with one of the pediatricians. Today I can see God's hand in even this small thing of which doctor we were to see that day. Dr. Reeves was a young doctor not long out of medical school. She had recently studied Kawasaki's Disease. She noticed symptoms that we did not. Knox had a red tongue and swollen feet as well, and his right lymph node in his neck was very large. She put these symptoms together to diagnose him with Kawasaki's. We were immediately sent to Children's Hospital.

Children's Hospital was not new to us, unfortunately. We'd made many visits for our four children over the years living in Omaha. I had also spent time there (days and weeks) with one of my closest friends who would lose two young babies to tragedy, a son at seven months and a daughter at nine months of age. I had experienced much loss at this hospital.

I had no idea about this "Kawasaki's" but I learned quickly that doctors took it very seriously. Knox was admitted immediately, and we had a whole swarm of doctors and nurses in and out of his room, attending to him. He was given a treatment of immunoglobulin medicine intravenously. As it goes, Garrick was out of town traveling on business. The first round of treatment did not work as they'd hoped, so I eventually requested Garrick return home early. Things were more serious than I could have guessed. This IVIG treatment needed to work because it was all they had to reset Knox's immune system. It seemed like it was attacking itself for reasons that are not medically understood.

The enemy, Satan, was there filling my head with lies. He wanted me to believe that because I was doing work for God's kingdom, the cost would be my son. I really had come to believe that lie as I sat there in the hospital next to Knox's bed, watching him suffering with this strange illness. Thank God that the Lord sent a friend to me, Krista, who came and boldly prayed over Knox and over me. She called out the lie for what it was. As she prayed, she said that she saw a picture of Knox as an adult preaching! He would be an evangelist for the Lord, and Satan would not stop this. Krista spoke truth into me and into this situation. Knox had his second birthday in the hospital. The staff there was really sweet to him, even singing the birthday song to him.

Creighton basketball players happened to make a visit the day of his birthday and even gave him a gift. We were not alone, I know that: God was right there seeing us through it. To confirm this, Knox pointed out to me angels that were in his room. He pointed to one corner behind him and said that there were two there. He pointed to the other corner of his room and said that there was another one standing there. I didn't know what to think of that at the time, but I was so thankful to know that Knox's life was firmly in God's hands. Knox responded well to the second round of IVIG and he was released after five overnights. We had some follow up appointments that confirmed that there was no lasting damage to his heart. He was healed!

In January of 2014, I was just beginning Whole Heart. Concurrently, plans with Valor seemed to be moving along. God had sent a special couple into the mix of things. Pastor Jay was an itinerant minister and his wife, Diane, was a teacher. They attended the weekly Valor planning meetings. Jay was able to share his own testimony with us of the various ways God had supernaturally provided for him and his wife. Jay was a spirit-led man of God. He had seen God move in ways I had never heard of. Jay suggested I connect with a lady named Jeni, who was a teacher working on her administrator's license. Jay knew her well and thought that she may be looking for a principal role in a Christian school.

I reached out to Jeni and she joined our planning group immediately. It felt like God had opened another door to make Valor a reality.

This was definitely a time of connections. One of those connections was with a man named Ty Schenzel. Years before I had attended a talk his wife, Terri, had given to our MOPS group. Then my husband and I had attended a Valentine's evening talk for couples with both Ty and Terri. I knew from those events that both Ty and Terri had huge hearts. God had called them years before to start a ministry serving North Omaha. It was called the Hope Center for Kids. It still operates today, serving at-risk youth in after school programs and also helping graduates build skills to improve employability.

I went to meet with Ty in late January 2014, along with one of our planning members named Nicole. It turned out that Ty had been called away due to an emergency, so we met with his admin named Teresa. She asked about the purpose for our visit, so we shared briefly about the vision for a school we were carrying. Her face lit up as she shared that that very morning, Ty had shared with his board a vision he had for starting an elementary school! It seemed like more than a coincidence to us at the time, and I still think it is. (At the time of this book, a school has not yet come to pass at the Hope Center.) I met with Ty several times after this day. He was incredibly encouraging and supportive of what we were trying to do. He carried God's heart and tremendous wisdom, having sacrificed much of his life to the cause God had given him.

Ty and Terri were tragically killed in August of 2015 in a head-on collision on Interstate 29 between the border of Iowa and South Dakota. This happened only after Ty had stepped away from oversight for the Hope Center. The leadership was in place to carry on the mission that Ty had dutifully fulfilled to the Lord to serve the least of these.

Garrick and I attended a memorial service for them at a church called Way Point which we had never been to before. We were moved by the presence of God that was obviously at work there. During the service, I had an experience in the spirit that I shared with Garrick on the way home and which I recorded in my journal later that night:

8.21.15
Today we found out that Ty and Terri Schenzel were killed in a car accident in South Dakota yesterday. Heartbreaking, Lord, but we know you have them.

Lifted Up

Thank you, Father, for releasing the marriage blessing over us that they carried. Tonight at the prayer service, I had the impression (saw in the spirit with my heart) that Ty and Terri were walking down the aisle together arm in arm. They came to our pew and leaned in and took our hands in theirs to bless us and hand us a baton. Yes, Lord. Bring Garrick and I into unity with the mantle you are giving us to carry. May it be all about heart and hope.

A few days later, the funeral was held. I listened to it online. I was taken by surprise when one of the pastors giving the eulogy held up a baton and referenced it. The Omaha World Herald gave this quote, "The Rev. Lincoln Murdoch waves a baton at the memorial service to challenge mourners to take over the race." The Schenzels, he said, "ran so well. They ran so hard. Now, the baton stands. Who will pick it up and run with it?""

That message by Rev. Murdoch was a special confirmation of what I had experienced at their memorial service. I prayed that God would cause both Garrick and I to step into all that He has for us in helping others, especially children and families, in our community and beyond. Garrick took the death of Ty and Terri extremely hard for reasons I didn't initially understand, but then God showed me how He was using their lives and their sudden death to do a work in Garrick's heart. Here is another journal entry from a couple of days later:

8.27.15 10:45pm
At lunch, Garrick was sharing his heart about the loss of The Schenzels. He has been consumed by videos of them, Ty's sermons, and Facebook messages. I had a strong impression of Jesus sitting next to Garrick with his arm around him. I felt like he said, "Can you see the work I'm doing in him?"

Then a little while later, I felt like Jesus got up and stood behind Garrick and placed this mantle on him, which looked to me like a horse yoke, strong and made of leather and oval-shaped. I heard

Jesus say "I've given Garrick the Fatherhood Mantle. This was the same mantle Ty wore."

Later I told Garrick that I'm not sure he gets the depth of significance of this.

My husband is a complicated fella. His heart is as big as anyone's I've ever met, and yet for most of his life he has kept his heart guarded. Much of Garrick's early life was defined by his own dad's mania. Nancy, Garrick's mom, met Jerry when she was just a teenager and he was her high school teacher. Jerry had been recently divorced and had a daughter from his first marriage. (Interestingly, we found out just a couple of years before Jerry died that he had also had a son whom he and his first wife had given up for adoption because they didn't feel that they could provide for him. This son, Jeff had spent years looking for his birth parents and had finally found Jerry and was able to reconnect with him. It was at this time that Garrick found out that he had an older half-brother! They were instantly connected and remain close to this day, especially in their mutual love of the Boston Redsox.)

At age 17, Nancy got pregnant with Garrick, and they chose the honorable thing in getting married, against the protest of Nancy's mom, Betty who was a single mother whose alcoholic ex-husband had abandoned her with 3 young children. Nancy undoubtedly was drawn to a father figure to fill the gap her absent father had left. There would be a division between Betty and Nancy that would span decades because of this child and marriage, but this too would be healed as Garrick became an adult. Garrick, born in 1970, grew up essentially as an only child of a young mother and a bipolar father who self-medicated with alcohol. From the stories Garrick has shared, Jerry was manic-depressive and could be quite violent. He would be up and then he would be down. Garrick's young life revolved around his dad's moods and temper. Jerry was an imposing figure at 6'4. Nancy, just a tiny thing at just over 5 foot, learned to keep her mouth shut to protect herself and Garrick the best she could against Jerry's unpredictable mood swings.

Lifted Up

When I met Garrick, one of the first things I admired about him was his ability to forgive. He opened up to me about the beatings he took as a child, the mental abuse, and about the isolation he grew up in as Nancy kept the world out due to shame and guilt. He told me that he had vowed in his heart to not continue on the legacy of abuse that his father had given to him, and that Jerry had received from his own father.

As I got to know Nancy and Jerry, I could see that Garrick really loved them and forgave them for what he had endured. He was able to have a pretty healthy relationship with them as an adult, though they never really talked about Jerry's past behavior or the profound impact it had on their lives for decades.

When Garrick was in college, he lived at home with his parents who both worked for the school. Dr. Gerald Baxter was a professor at North-west Missouri State, and Nancy worked in the Grant office. Jerry suffered a mental breakdown after being caught plagiarizing a publication. He lost his job under much scandal and threatened suicide. This difficult chapter in their life led Jerry to receive the help that he needed through counseling and medication.

Garrick would graduate from NW Missouri earning a bachelor's in Psychology, attempting to understand his father better. After college he ended up becoming a store manager for a little coffee company, Starbucks. At the time, they were just beginning to open up new markets. They moved Garrick to the East coast to open up stores in the Carolina's. After several years with Starbucks, he had had enough of retail sales and chose to move out to the West coast, to Portland, OR. He reconnected with his Gramma Betty who was living just a couple of hours south in Eugene. Garrick had lived in Portland 4 years when we met. By then, Garrick had found his way into the Digital Marketing arena which was just beginning to explode into relevance.

Garrick and I are cut from the same cloth in that both of us knew what it was to strive to earn love. We both knew what it was like to try to be what someone else needed us to be. We both knew crazy explosive parents who could wound us deeply with their words and steal our sense of safety with their choices. And, both our hearts are naturally tender. We are compassionate people by nature with a special appreciation for the vulnerability of children. We were meant to be parents, though neither of us was initially prepared for the sacrifice it would take to raise *healthy* children. Our own experiences growing up did not prepare us, but we've both been consistently open to learning and changing so that we can become the parents our kids deserve. We learn and grow daily, sometimes begrudgingly, and mostly through trial and error!

Back to the spring of 2014: Each person I would meet with would give me a few more names of people to connect with in my quest to start a Christian school in southwest Omaha. I had been put into contact with a Christian architect named Bob, who worked for BCDM architects. He had helped to scope out the potential land development at Nebraska Christian. He was helping with the potential partnership with the Presbyterian church. In the natural, there was so much to be done and I continued to strive under my own strength to try to move mountains.

I was progressing through Whole Heart. Pastor Chuck had recommended a resource on hearing God's voice by an author and speaker named Mark Virkler. Listening to Mark's CDs did help me to begin to discern God's voice amidst the noise of my own mind, or even the voice of the enemy, Satan, who can also enter into the conversation if our hearts are not guarded. This an excerpt from my notes written while listening to one of Mark's teachings. I would definitely recommend checking out for yourself the revelation Mark has been given by God about communicating with Him.

> We put thoughts into 3 different categories:
> 1. Spontaneous positive thoughts = Holy Spirit
>   Counselor, comforter, truth, teacher, edifier
> 2. Spontaneous negative thoughts = Demons/Satan
>   Liar, accuser, thief, adversary
> 3. Analytical thoughts = self

Lifted Up

(Mark's teaching referenced Ezekiel 14:4) My notes said: Getting rid of any idol in my heart. God gives the answer but in light of the idol in my heart-it will pass through the idol and get distorted.

> *"Therefore speak to them and tell them, 'This is what the Sovereign Lord says: When any of the Israelites set up idols in their hearts and put a wicked stumbling block before their faces and then go to a prophet, I the Lord will answer them myself in keeping with their great idolatry. "*
>
> Ezekiel 14:4

On this same day, I asked the Lord the following questions and this was what I heard from Him in response:

Lord what do you want to say to me?

"That I am here. That I love you. That I never leave you. Oh, why do you doubt me, my dear child? My plans are great, your place in those plans is secure. You are a leader. I will continue to bless you with the vision, but others will receive them too. You are to work together for my purposes with Valor. There is coming a time of great plenty. You will have all that you ask for to bless the children, trust in that, plan ahead and be wise with what I give to you, seek me in every decision great or small. I am walking with you on this journey. It will not be short, but will be plentiful in spirit for many years."

Lord, what do we need to understand right now with regards to money/tuition?

"That I have already provided for the families who will attend."

The next day, Garrick and I went to a place in Omaha called The Hub. It is a prophetic gathering place founded by Juliane Christensen. It was our first visit and we didn't know what to expect.

It was recommended to us by a friend, so we went there for our "date night". We met a man named Marcus and ended up praying with him. That night Garrick had a closed vision. (A closed vision is where a person can see something with their mind's eye playing out internally. This is different from an open vision, where a person sees with their physical eyes a scene that is going on in the spiritual realm.)

Garrick didn't want to share it at first. It brought tears to his eyes. He said that it will "blow me away". When he was ready to share, he said that, "Valor is not meant just for Omaha. It's supposed to be repeatable all over the U.S." In the vision, he said that he saw himself giving out money, grants, or something. Pastor Jay said that when he prayed for Valor, he kept seeing more than one location too, so what Garrick shared was just a confirmation.

At the end of February 2014, we held an event at Nebraska Christian College to bring together the families who we knew were interested. At that point, we were thinking that the Presbyterian Church location might be a temporary location for us while we built a permanent school on the Nebraska Christian campus. I asked the Lord about the purpose of this event and this was what I heard:

> "Tonight, let it be about each family I have called. Remind them to tune to me. Remind them that it was I that gave them their children, and that I have a special purpose for each of them. I have called you, and each of them, and more, to this mission. They are to support it, in every way, telling their neighbors about it, sharing the good news. Valor will be amazing because I will be there. I will live there with the children."

On February 28th, my birthday, we received word that Faith Church had approved a partnership with Valor. This was the scripture the Lord sent me to that evening:

Lifted Up

"Now to him who is able to do immeasurably more than all we ask or imagine, according to his power that is at work within us, [21] to him be glory in the church and in Christ Jesus throughout all generations, for ever and ever! Amen."   *Ephesians 3:20-21*

I breathed a sigh of relief. I thought things must be coming together. We had yet to raise any money, but I trusted God for the promises I had heard Him speak to me.

3.2.14

My Lord and King, reveal to me one powerful and crazy thing:

"You will be given $10M to plant seeds."

Please show me where I am holding onto something prideful:

"Your heart holds onto what it knows. I am beyond your knowing. What I can do has never been experienced before. Stop limiting me. Don't fear about fundraising. Yes, you will have to humble yourself to ask for resources, but it will not be you asking, it is I. I will direct you who you need to go to, I will give you the words. They will respond in the way I've directed them. There is no such thing as failure. You are obedient. That is all I ask of you. I love you, little lamb."

"Don't fear leading others either. Hand out assignments, build people up. Hug, encourage, care for your team. Yes, they are your team. You are their leader. It's okay. That is not prideful. Seek me in every decision and I will be there."

3.9.14

God is so good. He is going to do something amazing for Valor. Tonight, I got the verse from Matthew about the temple tax that the king doesn't have his children pay, but instead his servants. Perhaps we won't be charging tuition... God is going to give us $10m to sow seeds.

My Whole Hearted Testimony

This morning during the first church service, I heard a word that confirmed something for me: I am to surrender my life's work to God. He will write my story and it will be better than anything I could ever dream. I always thought that I would be a process improvement person... I never dreamed God would have me start a Christian school, a Christian community.

Lord, thank you for bringing me through this weekend, more whole, and more filled with you. I love you Lord God, king of my life. You are beautiful and upright. My all and all.

"Rest. Allow me to prepare you in heart, mind, and spirit."

A couple of days later, I was praying at work. This is what I recorded:

3.11.14
The Lord gave me a scripture to look up:

"He told her, "Go, call your husband and come back."" John 4:16

Who knew there was a scripture like that in the Bible that instructed a wife to call her husband?! I thought that seemed like clear instruction, so I did as I was directed. I tried to call Garrick but it went to voicemail. I later found that he was on an airplane in mid-flight. I decided to text him instead. I figured that was okay. There weren't texting capabilities 2000 years ago when John wrote that scripture, but if there were, I was sure he would be fine with it!

I texted Garrick that God had sent me to that scripture. He responded back to me, "So do I have a message or do you?" Hmmm, I didn't know. I prayed and asked God what He would have me tell Garrick. I emailed him this message:

I love you so much, Garrick. You are all that I could have ever wished for in a husband, in the father for my children. You are a man of God. I thank God for you.

God wants you to know that He loves you. That you are right where you are supposed to be. That there is nothing to fear. Seek Him. Listen for Him. Follow Him. Pour out your heart to Him, because it is His heart. You are all that He made you to be. You are everything you need to be. There is nothing you are lacking.

Let your heart expand to take Him in. Follow Him. It may not make sense where He is leading you but trust. At just the right moment, He will give you the words. You will speak them. You will feel that they aren't from you. You will feel a warmth, an uprising. A confusion, but a peace. His work flows through you.

The purpose of this trip is not what you thought it is. It is more. His plans are always greater than our plans. Don't fear. Don't worry. Be calm and confident in Him. You are greater than you know, because He is in you. Trust.

Garrick responded with this:

"I know why you're supposed to call me. I prayed last night that your job would end. I considered the loss of great money, but the extra money is such a hassle. It's not worth it to our kids and our marriage. I wondered today how long I would be able to tell you. God found me out in less than eighteen hours."

Garrick and I talked and we agreed that God meant for me to quit my job. I asked the Lord to give me a supporting scripture. (It is always best to ask God to confirm what we thought we heard with His Word, the Bible. This method has never let me down. God is faithful to answer!

If the scripture I am sent to does not line up with what I am believing, then I know I need to wait on God because I may have missed something in translation.) God sent me to Daniel 4:14,

> *He called in a loud voice: 'Cut down the tree and trim off its branches; strip off its leaves and scatter its fruit. Let the animals flee from under it and the birds from its branches. Daniel 4:14*

The context of this chapter in Daniel is that King Nebuchadnezzar has a dream that greatly disturbs him. None of his other magicians can interpret the dream so he calls for Daniel to give the interpretation. Daniel understood the meaning but doesn't want to tell him because it is a hard word. Basically, God is telling Nebuchadnezzar that if he doesn't repent, all will be taken from him.

This is what Daniel tells him in verses 24-27:

> "*This is the interpretation, Your Majesty, and this is the decree the Most High has issued against my lord the king: [25] You will be driven away from people and will live with the wild animals; you will eat grass like the ox and be drenched with the dew of heaven. Seven times will pass by for you until you acknowledge that the Most High is sovereign over all kingdoms on earth and gives them to anyone he wishes.*

> [26] *The command to leave the stump of the tree with its roots means that your kingdom will be restored to you when you acknowledge that Heaven rules. [27] Therefore, Your Majesty, be pleased to accept my advice: Renounce your sins by doing what is right, and your wickedness by being kind to the oppressed. It may be that then your prosperity will continue.*"

Well, Nebuchadnezzar did not turn from his sins and twelve months later, while he was basking in his own glory, a voice came from heaven and announced,

> "*Even as the words were on his lips, a voice came from heaven,*

Lifted Up

"This is what is decreed for you, King Nebuchadnezzar: Your royal authority has been taken from you.

32 You will be driven away from people and will live with the wild animals; you will eat grass like the ox. Seven times will pass by for you until you acknowledge that the Most High is sovereign over all kingdoms on earth and gives them to anyone he wishes."
Daniel 4:31-32

What I heard from this was that I was not to be the provider, the generous one. God is to be the provider. All our needs will be met through him. I do not need to provide financially for Valor, because He will.

It's been over five years since I received this message from the Lord, which seemed so clear at the time. I wish that I could say that I had been completely obedient to this command, but I cannot. I did plan to leave the job and even turned in my notice. But then, some things happened with Garrick's professional life, and we agreed that I needed to continue to work for a period of time. Thankfully, God has been merciful to me. He has not put me out to pasture like He did to Nebuchadnezzar, though I may have deserved it!

As if my plate was not full enough with four children, a high-stress job, Garrick's changing work situation, and planning for a school... we were having a lake house built. Seriously, even as I type all those things out, I think how could I have been so optimistic about my ability to carry all those things? If *God* were carrying all those things at that point, I would have been fine. *We* would have been fine. **But I was not yet allowing God to carry much of anything.** Though my heart was whole for the first time in my life, I did not yet know how to live without striving. I was incredibly driven. I did not sit still. I could not sit still. Literally I was in motion, unless I was physically asleep.

I had spent months planning out the Beaver lake house. I had designed it myself using a little iPad app. I had laid in bed at night for hours and hours, dreaming about this house. At the time, I was blinded by my own dream. I believed that God wanted to bless us. As I labored for His Kingdom, surely He wanted us to be blessed. I also wanted the lake house to be a blessing to my mom. She was close to retirement age. We had worked out a deal where she covered the down payment for the house, and Garrick and I would cover the ongoing mortgage payments. This allowed her to retire a little bit early. She had always wanted to live on a lake. It seemed like a perfect arrangement.

This was a season in my life where the Lord really wanted to teach me about listening to Him first, then taking steps of faith according to His lead. This was so opposite to how I had operated up until that time. I have to tell you, I failed often. I failed big. But in my failure, God has brought beautiful things to life in me and through me.

The Beaver Lake dream would eventually die a very painful and bloody death. After reducing my consulting hours, and with money going to Valor, we just couldn't afford a second house. This caused a major chasm between me and my mom. I hurt her and I hurt my sisters, who were also involved in the transaction. I needed to acknowledge that I made a mistake, a big one. I ran out in front of God and gave birth to an Ishmael! (If you don't know that analogy, I encourage you to read Genesis Chapters 15 through 18.)

Just because I recognized my mistake and said that I was sorry did not mean that I received immediate forgiveness. My sin of pride and selfishness in this situation hurt my relationship with my family. I am thankful to be able to say that my sisters and my mom were able to eventually forgive me. Thank God for their love and His grace!

4am - Early morning of 3.14.14

I'm laying here this early morning listening to God. I asked what we should do with Faith Pres. I feel like God responded with:

"Walk away from Faith church".

I was reflecting on how the Faith church option came to be. I felt "led" there immediately following my meeting with Teri Lynn. I was so excited to be presented another church option that I went right over there. I did not pray on it. And then Pastor Mark was gracious about it and the process with them began. It seemed so perfect to me. But there has been much heartache and uncertainty.

Even yesterday when Mitch and I met with them and the architects, they brought up a facilities meeting they had, where it got heated and there was more opposition and the suggestion that the topic of a school would need to go in front of the church to be voted on. Jerry, their ops guy, restated that the board approved a feasibility study only as the next step. Even how he shared this seemed to be in a different context then I heard before. He shared that they got a quote for additional cleaning each month that would be needed and it was $1,100 just for that, with other monthly expenses of $531. We didn't think we could afford that much. What I thought was a foregone conclusion was not. People in their church were asking,– 'Why should we change our church to accommodate a school that is only going to be here a short time?

I hear that I am not seeking God first in every decision, great or small. And our location is one of the few great and defining decisions. When I sought God in it today, I heard "walk away" so clearly.

Jay told me a story a couple of days ago. He and his wife had been trying to conceive for ten years. They heard from the Lord that she would become pregnant, so she resigned her teaching position, then she got pregnant. She didn't wait until after she WAS pregnant. It was an act of faith. What is rattling around is that an act of faith was demonstrated, and God provided.

My greatest desire is to be obedient to God. His plan for Valor is better than any plan I could conceive.

My Whole Hearted Testimony

I just asked for another scripture and God gave me John 14:8 - Phillip said, "*Lord, show us the Father and that will be enough for us*". Jesus goes on to admonish Phillip for not seeing that He is the Father. From this, I hear that Jesus is directing us and I am not acknowledging that direction.

Praise God! He is here with us now. He has left the Holy Spirit here with us so that we are never apart. What joy!

8:44am – I'm rereading the above from 4 a.m. when it was way too early for me to be awake, Lord Jesus, my Savior and Redeemer. You are always with me. I feel your loving kindness poured out on me. You are my strength and my shield against all trouble. Jesus, I pray that you would help me to understand what I have not been seeing clearly.

"I just wanted to be with you. There are times when I have something I want to share with you to direct you, but I just want to be in your heart. I love you, Rachel, my little lamb, white as snow. You are lovely to me. I am your love. Slow down. Breathe. I will meet all your needs, and then some! It doesn't have to be as hard as you are making it. You can't get this wrong. You are seeking me and I will direct you, your every action if you desire it.

Thank you for inviting me to that deep special place that exists only for you and I. The more you yield to me, the greater the vision will become, and the clearer it will become. There is nothing hidden from you. I desire you to understand and trust in the path I have set forth. No fear, no worry. The place will be perfect for the first time, and then you will be led to the next place and it will be what it is meant to be for My glory. The little children will come to me. Focus on them. Focus on where they are today and where I desire them to be tomorrow. I have prepared a place where my sheep listen to me, where they seek to do my will. This is not at Faith Church. Do not worry about these people. They are mine, too.

Lifted Up

The time is drawing near when you will have all the resources you need for Valor, and also for your family. There is nothing you need to do to MAKE that happen. I will make that happen. It is my gift to you. Hear my voice. It is also my Father's. We are one and we invite you into our presence now and for eternity. Feel my presence right now."

Then the Lord sent me to this scripture:

"Be careful that you do not forget the Lord, who brought you out of Egypt, out of the land of slavery. "   Deuteronomy 6:12

Later in the day, I communicated what I felt like I had heard from the Lord to the Valor planning team. They prayed on it with me and we all felt like the Lord was guiding us to walk away from partnership with Faith Church. We trusted that God's hand was guiding us. We believed that He would lead us to where we were meant to open the school. It was helpful to me also to have people around me that were willing to seek God and hold me accountable for what I was hearing.

One day when I was driving in to work, I saw a sign on a Dino Storage building near Midtown Omaha that said, "There is safety in many counselors." How true. God doesn't just speak to me. He speaks to any person who seeks Him.

That is not to say that we are to trust any person who says they are hearing from God. We need to take everything back to Him ourselves and seek confirmation or rebuttal. I believe Holy Spirit is so good to answer our prayers through peace in our spirit or through discontent. At least, that is how it works for me!

This is the lesson: when we follow the Lord alone and let him number our steps and light our path, we cannot fail and the victory is His.

If I will do my part, trusting that I can hear His voice and follow Him, I cannot fail. I do my part and trust Him with the outcome. I must not

My Whole Hearted Testimony

take on the outcome, or else the glory would be mine and not His. The Lord gave me specific instructions about my job. I was to stop working but I chose not to listen. Together with my husband, we came up with the best plan that we could. And, the next four years were extremely hard for me as I tried to carry Valor financially by continuing to do consulting work, while *trying* to lead Valor on a part-time basis when full-time leadership was God's best.

The Lord did not tell me to go to Faith church, so I spent months striving to make something happen that was not meant to be. The Lord did not tell me to run off to build a second house on the lake! And so I spent months of blood, sweat, and tears trying to make something happen, only to have to give up that dream.

I've made mistakes–some pretty big— and the reality is that those mistakes have hurt people. I know that I've hurt my husband most of all. The changes in me have been dramatic, I'm sure causing him whiplash at times. It has been a wild ride, and our lives have been dramatically impacted by choices I made apart from God, and apart from honoring my husband too.

I truly believe if I would have stopped and listened to God with each of those situations, things could have turned out differently–better. I know that it is okay that I made mistakes. God's grace covers all. But His heart for me is that I would learn from those mistakes, just as we, as parents, long for our children to learn from the mistakes they make.

I desperately want to be who God created me to be. He has placed a deep burning inside of me to let go of the things of this world and embrace His plans for me. But I need to recognize that because I do not fully understand God's ways, if I lean on my own understanding, I'm likely going to get it wrong. I *need* God to teach me. I *need* to learn to wait on God for His wisdom to come forward. I *need* to ask Him to give me patience, which is one of the fruits of the Spirit!

Lifted Up

I need to demonstrate the fruit of the spirit in my relationships with others—patience, kindness, and gentleness especially, recognizing that each person is on their own journey and place with God.

The more I learn about God and His ways, the more I come to understand who I am. Apart from Him, I am lost in this world. This is because He never intended one of His children to live apart from Him. If you can relate to my journey in some way... if you have ever run ahead of God, or if you have caused an Ishmael to be birthed, today is the perfect day to acknowledge your mistakes to God on High, who is also an intimate God who delights in every part of His creation.

Step of Faith:

Here is a challenge for you -

Ask God to show you choices that you have made apart from Him. Where have you run ahead of God? When have you chosen your own dreams, instead of asking God to give you the desires of His heart?

I believe He will reveal these things to you because He loves you and delights in who He made you to be. He has not left you even for one moment, and there is no decision you could ever make apart from Him that cannot be redeemed.

Then, ask Him to forgive you for each mistake. Place the mistake under the cross covered by Jesus blood. Ask Jesus to come into the situation and redeem it for His purposes, for your good. Lastly, ask the Lord to help you surrender all your dreams to Him. Ask Him to place His dream predestined before time began into your heart. He is good and faithful to do just that!

Lifted Up

CHAPTER 7: I'm a Good, Good Father

At this point in the journey, the Valor planning committee continued to meet weekly. Progress was being made on all fronts... except where we were to open. I was trying desperately to find a new building, driving around the southwest part of the city, trying to follow zoning maps that seemed to be written in Greek. I was striving under my own strength; and despite my best efforts, I was coming up empty.

I searched out church after church, with doors remaining closed to me, afraid of failure. I felt the burden of all these people, teachers, and families relying on me. I should have been relying on God and pointing them to God, but I wasn't. I should have been focused on what God had provided, his people, instead of what he had not provided, a place.

3.22.14:05pm
Lord, I am weary but I feel Your presence and truth. I pray that you would protect me, Garrick, and our children from any stronghold, from the enemy. May we all see your truth and cling to it. Please see the vision you've given Garrick for Devoto (an S Corp Garrick was trying to launch) to fruition, and also the vision for Valor. I pray that you would give us a building and soon Lord, so that we can advertise and promote. I pray for your abundant financial blessing on Valor. Fill our bank account, Lord. I praise you for Your mercy. I love you, Lord. Thank you for being with us today at the prayer service. What a wonderful testament to you. Thank you for each family and each child that came, and that you are calling to Valor.

I trust you Lord. I follow you. I am giving up my own life to follow. Please show me how I can have balance in my life and still serve you. Bring Garrick and I together.

"Rachel, do not fear that you don't hear me correctly. I am as clear as I desire to be. You get what I give to you. You are on the right path. I did not promise that it would be easy, but plentiful in

Spirit for many years. I will provide for every need Valor has at just the right time. It won't be in your time and there is nothing you can do to speed that timing up. Breathe. Be patient. Trust. Listen and really hear.

You need to relinquish some of your power. You were right today, thinking of reorganizing with Jeni leading the school effort. That is not for you to do. You will oversee the operations. You do not need to respond to families. Heidi can do that. You do not need to take care of banking of funds. Heidi can do that. You do not need to lose time with recreating the filing docs. Relinquish control.

Ask Heidi. It is supposed to be a team effort. I will give you a building. Wait on The Lord, but praise me now because it has been done. Act as if. My spirit is with you. There is power. Learn to trust the authority. I will comfort you. You do less, I do more. I don't need all your time, just your first fruits. Think about your son. You would do anything for him. You are that to me. Just be in me. Sweet child. I love your heart. I have your soul. Focus on me. Tomorrow, see the lady with the purple hat. Go up to her and introduce yourself. Listen to her story and look in her eyes. She is the one at the well that needs to give you water. She needs to give it more than you need to receive it. Be receptive to her gift. It will be the first of many. The fountain begins to flow. Don't worry about getting your hopes up. You have been steadfast with the big things and I will be with everything. I hold you and your family in the palm of my hands."

As I re-read those entries, there are some clear messages to be found. God was speaking wisdom to me about actually laying down the control so that He could lead me. **He was encouraging me to learn to *rest*.** This was a major area of challenge for me. I had just not ever learned to truly rest–mind, body, and spirit. He was extending an invitation to me, but I wasn't allowing His olive branch to reach my heart.

Lifted Up

Interestingly enough, I would find myself crying out to the Lord 4 years later still desiring to learn how to rest. On the morning of January 23rd, 2018, lying in bed just waking up for the day I prayed this simple prayer: "Lord, cause me to come into your rest." Let me warn you against praying that prayer right now, unless you are ready for the answer!

That same afternoon, after we had called off school due to a snow storm that passed through earlier that morning, I drove to Valor with my kiddos to attend an impromptu staff meeting. I had taken one trip into the building and was returning to the van to grab a second load of stuff that I needed for the meeting when I slipped and my right foot slid and then caught on the ice. My foot stopped but my body kept going over. I fell onto the ice and felt the break in my right outside ankle bone.

I literally cried out to the Lord in pain and desperation. I knew that He could heal me in that moment, but He did not. My kids heard me crying and jumped out of the van with their own tears of fear. In the mania of the moment, I yelled at them to pray for me so that God would heal me! I could NOT have a broken ankle. I did NOT have time for that. I had so much to do and so many people relying on me. Didn't God realize that? My daughter, Emmelia, turned out to be level-headed under the pressure. She found my phone and called Julie, a Valor parent and friend who lived nearby. I couldn't get off the ground. I just layed there helpless and vulnerable shivering on the ice. It wasn't long and Julie arrived on the scene and determined that an ambulance would be needed.

With tears streaming down my face, and firetruck sirens blowing, the EMT's loaded me into the ambulance. Even in that moment, God found a way to encourage me. An EMT pointed out a bald eagle flying overhead. Never before or again have I seen an eagle over the school. Yes, He was there, watching over me. I do not believe that the Lord caused my fall or my ankle to break, but He did bring good out of it. I was laid up for 12 weeks with not much I could physically do except to rest. During that time, I was given a gift.

My Whole Hearted Testimony

It was time that I realize in the core of my being that my value did not come from what I do or accomplish. The first few days I cried and grumbled to the Lord who had allowed this seemingly terrible thing to happen to me. But then something began to shift in my heart. Day by day the world went on around me. It just kept spinning and all I could do was observe.

And yet, I began to believe the truth that my life was still *valuable* even in the absence of actions.

What I was shown was that although I could not do the housework or make the meals, my presence in our family was still critical. I began to see my children differently without the distraction of busyness. I watched them interacting with each other. I watched them happily taking on mom's chores delighting in serving me. I saw them in a new way and I realized that I could still meet their needs through the love and patience I showed them. And by serving me in my time of need, they gained confidence and surprised even themselves in what they were capable of doing from the laundry to dishes to meal prep.

I was basically out of Valor for 3 months and somehow things continued to hum along. Things that really needed to get done got done. Children continued to learn and grow, and the other Valor staff were given the opportunity to blossom in their own gifts and abilities in my absence, allowing the Lord to use them to meet each need.

During that time, I listened to a David Wilkerson teaching from years ago. In his sermon, he shared that the Lord had shown him that true rest means that we recognize that God has made a seat for us at His table in the heavens and that we choose to take our seat. We sit with Him. We operate only from the place of authority He already gave us, bought through the price Jesus paid.

To clarify, I learned that true rest in the Lord is not a physical concept. To rest in Him means that I allow my strength to come from Him. Resting in Him means that I can be weak and allow Him to be strong.

Lifted Up

How often do we continue on a course of action even when something in us tells us that it is futile? Come on! I know I can't be the only one who defaults to striving under my own strength towards an outcome. I believe that God wants us to see the finish line, but we have no strength left to make it to the end on our own. He wants us to need Him, to seek Him, to reach out to Him, so that He can carry us. He desires to propel us forward to victory. Well, I wasn't quite getting the message fully in the spring of 2014.

I was feeling overwhelmed by all the facets of the school launch. The Lord was so good to give me clear instructions of what to let go of. I am happy to say that upon the next meeting, I shared this 'God encounter' and humbled myself enough to ask for help in the areas I had received instruction about. And to my surprise, Jeni and Heidi were happy to help and felt like they had the time to do what needed to be done. Wow—you mean I didn't need to try to do everything by myself? Crazy!

It's not really. Why should it surprise us when people want to help us? Don't most of us appreciate the opportunity to help others when we can? Of course. I believe it is just a terrible lie that we believe: that if something is going to get done, we need to do it ourselves. Our God is a God of relationships. He created us for relationship with Him and with each other. So wouldn't it stand to perfect reason that God would be glorified through working together towards a common purpose? Yes!

You might have noticed the somewhat strange directions about the "lady with the purple hat". The Lord would give me instructions like this quite often during this time. I believe His intention was that I would begin to really listen to what He was saying and trust Him for under-standing. He knew that my favorite game as a child was Clue. I love a good mystery! My brain thrives on putting puzzle pieces together, so God would send me on little missions of obedience, day by day. I didn't see a woman with a purple hat the next day, though that doesn't mean that she hadn't walked by, but there were many times I would see what God had directed me to look for.

One example of this was when the Lord told me to look for a man in a plaid shirt at work. The next day, I think I saw ten men wearing plaid shirts and didn't have peace about going up to <u>any</u> of them. The Lord was highlighting to me the fear of man that I carried, and continued to battle for some time.

Have you ever been nervous to speak up in a large group, or to go up an introduce yourself to a stranger? Well, me too. Why is this? Could it be that we are afraid of how other people will respond to us? What if we are rejected? I had a fear of rejection that the Lord desired to deal with. Fear is never from God.

> "For God hath not given us the spirit of fear; but of power, and of love, and of a sound mind."   *2 Timothy 1:7 KJV*

So, if fear doesn't come from God, then it must come from Satan. It is a great pleasure of Satan's to cause fear in our hearts. Fear keeps us from doing and saying things that may advance the Kingdom of God. For us to walk in the fullness of who we are as children of God, we must conquer fear in our lives.

The truth is this: if I am trusting in God to meet all my needs, to be my protector and provider in all circumstances, then man has no power over me. Satan has no power over me. There is nothing I can't do through the Lord within His will.

God was sending me on little missions of obedience—to build my trust in Him and continue to refine my hearing as well. He also wanted to show me that when I am walking with Him, I get to release His Kingdom. What does that look like?

It may look like just encouraging someone who is having a rough day. It may also look like making a deep connection with a total stranger. People walk around every day, feeling so broken and alone. It is rare that someone takes the chance to break into someone else's box they've built around themselves, to make a connection. Am I right?

Lifted Up

When was the last time someone outside your close circle of friends or family touched your heart? When was the last time you went out on a limb to really help someone you didn't know well?

What I have found is that the more I give my mind to the Lord, the more He will direct me into someone else's path—for a purpose. I've found that it is actually easier for me to go up to a complete stranger to speak truth into his/her life than it is for me to speak truth into one of my own immediate family member's lives. Why is that? Could it be that silly old fear of rejection again? Ugh.

I've lost track of the number of times God has sent me on a simple two-minute mission to brighten someone's day. My kids have gotten used to "mom's little side trips". They usually happen in a parking lot or the aisle of a store. The scenario usually goes something like this: God will point someone out to me. He will tell me to go up and talk to them. I will argue in my head with God, trying to tell Him why they wouldn't want to hear from me or that they must be too busy and don't want to be interrupted. He will tell me again what He is asking me to do. I will then try to talk myself into it and then back out of it again. I wish I could say that I obey automatically every time, but I don't. Sometimes my own mission to accomplish a task gets in my way. Other times my own heart just isn't positioned to be able to pour out. But when I do obey, I am always the one who is blessed in the encounter, because I get to impact someone by bringing a simple message of love from the Lord into their day.

The more I obey, the easier it becomes because I see God working. I am always surprised and relieved when the person He asks me to speak to is kind to me. I shouldn't be surprised, though. I've actually never been told to shut up, so that is a good sign! What I've found is that most people are open to hearing me out. Most people are so deeply in need of a touch from God, even just a simple word from a regular person like me, that they are open to receiving.

I've learned from God, and through wise teachers who minister in the prophetic, that words from God will never hurt. God will never ask a person to share a word with someone else that will bring personal condemnation. That might not jive with your theology so let me clarify. I am not talking about prophetic words of judgment that God **DOES** release to a people group to bring them back to repentance before Him. I'm referring to personal prophetic messages from one person to another.

I am talking about a word of knowledge or message for a specific person. God's words always bring life. They do not bring death. Now, Satan loves to twist words to bring death. That is why we have to be aware of the state of our own heart before we release a word to someone else. If my heart is hurting, or if I am believing a lie or if I have been offended and not worked through those things with the Lord, my heart is open to hearing the enemy as well as God. If I am hearing the enemy, I could very well release a word to someone else that would hurt them or cause further damage to their heart.

The first part of 2 Corinthians 13:5 states this:

> *"Examine yourselves to see whether you are in the faith; test yourselves. Do you not realize that Christ Jesus is in you—unless, of course, you fail the test?"*

This is why ongoing forgiveness and repentance, (using the Whole Heart model I laid out before) is so critical. If my heart is whole, I can receive what God is speaking. I am positioned to be used by Him to love others.

I learned that what God was teaching me to walk in was called the Gift of Prophecy mentioned in 1 Corinthians in 12:10. Often, God gives me pictures that appear in my mind's eye that are meant for someone else. Sometimes, I actually see a word that appears to be written on a person, on their forehead of chest for example.

Once, while at a OneThing Conference through IHOP in Kansas City, I saw a man walking down the aisle with the word "DROSS" written on his chest in bold letters. I did not know what the word meant. I felt prompted to go up to him to share this word. He had stopped to talk with another man. I approached and introduced myself. I then told him about seeing this word on his chest. His friend looked it up while I was talking. He said the word meant, "scum formed on the surface of something."

Well, that didn't sound too kind at first glance, but immediately the Lord spoke to me and told me to share with the man that the Lord was working to remove the dross from his life so that he could be purified and drawn closer to His creator. This touched the man and he received this openly.

When I see words that appear to be *on* someone, I am seeing in the Spirit. Sometimes I see things on or around people. I was once meeting with a Valor missionary also named Rachel. As she sat across from me talking, all of a sudden I saw black marks appear on her face. I asked the Lord what I was seeing and heard "war paint". I shared this word with her. She told me that this encouraged her greatly, because the Lord had been teaching her about what it is to war in the Spirit.

God just wants me to share what He is showing me. When I was beginning to share these things, I felt like I was going to screw it up. I thought the other person would think that I was just making something up. The enemy tried to tell me all kinds of lies to keep me from walking in the prophetic gifting that had come from God. It has been so critical for the Lord to also hone my gift of discernment. I must be able to discern whether what I am seeing in the spirit is from the Lord or from Satan.

I don't know if this is true for everyone who sees in the Spirit, but for me, I see good and evil in the spirit. I have learned that when I see a demonic spirit attached to someone, which is not as uncommon as you might think, that it is better NOT to tell the person! However, I can pray for that person and ask the Lord to show me what hurt has opened the door, which gives Satan the legal right to attach one of his minions to this person to bring them more pain and sorrow. If the opportunity arises, there are times I am able to speak truth into a person releasing the truth of God's love into their life, shining a light into the dark places where evil tries to hide. This is a form of deliverance where a person can be set free from their spiritual afflictions to experience freedom in the Lord.

Why would God ask me to give someone else a message from Him? It could be that they aren't listening at the time but that I am. I believe that God is always speaking, but so often we aren't listening. The God I have come to know is always working to grow closer to His children. He relentlessly pursues each of us, and won't pass up an opportunity to bless us. He will use anyone, even me and even you, to show His love to a son or daughter – especially a lost son or daughter.

Often, the people God directs me to don't look like Miss or Mr. America. They are people who look tired and weary. They are people who wear the signs of abuse or neglect on their bodies. They might be tattooed from head to toe or pierced up one side and down the other. But God loves every one of them. He really does.

Here are some statements God commonly has me share, though each encounter is different and special. He will tell me to say, "God loves you." "You are precious to God." "God has never left you even for a moment." "He catches every tear." "There is no mistake in you." "You are beautiful, inside and out." "God delights in your heart." "He is for you and not against you."

These statements reflect the true nature of God's heart for His children.

What do you think when you read these statements? Do you believe God would say things like this to you? Or do you instead believe you would hear a voice of condemnation for the mistakes you have made? It has not been easy for me to accept these kind of statements from God made to me. I've shared some of my past with you. The truth is that I did not experience unconditional love from my own earthly father. We tend to put characteristics of our earthly fathers onto God, but this is a mistake.

God loves us absolutely unconditionally. Even if I never did another thing *for* God again, He would still love me fully. Take that in a moment. It is true. There is nothing you must do for God to love you. This is truth. Yet, this is so opposite to the way the world works and what it teaches.

In my life, I had learned that if I do things for people, or if I act the way they want me to, or if I perform a certain way, then I will be loved. I believed that I was not enough on my own. I was somehow lacking something. My own father had left me when I was a little girl and has been essentially absent from my life since then. How then can Father God love me?

There is a song called "Good, Good Father" made famous by Chris Tomlin. The lyrics go like this:

"You're a good good father
It's who you are, it's who you are, it's who you are
And I'm loved by you
It's who I am, it's who I am, it's who I am..."

The first few times I heard this song, I had a really hard time singing these lyrics. Could this really be true? Is God really a good, good Father? I didn't know what that would look like, since my own Father didn't model that kind of love and devotion in my life.

Because sin entered this world, we do not experience the goodness of God as He intended it from creation. He is our Father and we are His sons and daughters, but He will never force Himself of us. If I am not walking in His will for my life, or the people in my life are not walking in His will but walking in sin, then our experience can be that of hurt, which is caused by sin from the evil one. Because this world is currently under the power of Satan, experiencing evil through pain and sorrow is common.

My Whole Hearted Testimony

"We know that we are children of God, and that the whole world is under the control of the evil one."   *1 John 5:19*

However, I believe that God wants us to recognize that His goodness is always available to us. What does the Bible say about God's goodness? Here are just a few Biblical references but there are many more.

"Give thanks to the LORD, for he is good;
his love endures forever."
Psalms 107:1

"How abundant are the good things
that you have stored up for those who fear you,
that you bestow in the sight of all,
on those who take refuge in you. "
Psalms 31:19

"Afterward the Israelites will return and seek the Lord their God and David their king. They will come trembling to the Lord and to his blessings in the last days."   *Hosea 3:5*

If God is really good, then as I lay down my life before Him, I should begin to experience His goodness more and more, right? Yes! I have found this tenant to be true. The more I learn about Him, the more I see how "at odds" His nature is with this fallen world. God is so good that He gave His only son to redeem us.

"For God so loved world that he gave his one and only Son, that- whoever believes in him shall not perish but have eternal life."
John 3:16

This is not a cliché. This is the best example of His goodness towards His creation. After my college years of falling away from faith, I vividly re-member hearing the following scripture from Romans 5 and thinking through the ramifications of this for my life.

Lifted Up

"But God demonstrates his own love for us in this: While we were still sinners, Christ died for us." Romans 5:8

God didn't wait to save me or start to love me once I turned from my life of sin to Him. It wasn't in my own goodness that God demonstrated His goodness. It was in my weakness that God's goodness shone through. While I was still a sinner, Jesus laid down his life for me. The Lord reminded me of this again just today as I was on a walk. He said to me, *"You know Rachel, Jesus would have died just for you."* Just for me Lord? Wow, now that is love.

Would you give your life for one of your children? I believe that I would. Well, God is no different. He is a good, good Father. He doesn't love us only in our obedience. I believe from God's vantage point, He sees who He created us to be, not who we are in this particular moment—which might look like a hot mess full of mistakes, pride, selfishness, etc.

When I began to receive the revelation of God's goodness, His unchanging love for me, my life began to change. If God could love me no matter what, then maybe I could learn to love myself no matter what. **If God saw me according to who He made me to be, then maybe He could teach me to see myself for who He created me to be, not as the sum of my shortcomings on any given day.**

If I could begin to live out of the assurance of God's goodness for me, then perhaps I could overcome the greatest struggle of my life—performance. Because I thought I had to accomplish something to be loved or to be valued, I didn't know how to live out of a place of acceptance for who I was (created to be).

4.4.14
Lord, please show me where Valor is meant to be located.

"Rachel, dear child, sweet child... I love you. I cherish our time and I hope you do, too. Don't ask me what is not yours to know yet. At the right time, it will be revealed and it will be perfect.

Patience, grasshopper! Until then, meditate on my word: John 4:7."

Jesus asks the Samaritan woman if she will give him water to drink.

Yes, Jesus. I will give you anything that you ask. I ask you to give me living water in you that I will never thirst again.

You can see my single-mindedness to find a site for the school, can't you? But, do you see how good God was during this time? He never missed an opportunity while my ears were tuned to Him to encourage me, to point me to truth, to show His goodness to me.

4.8.14 9:46pm

Father, what did you show Boston last night?

"I am with you. I am. I am building my school. I am building my kingdom. My house has many rooms. My kingdom come. My will be done, today and every day. I dwell in you, in my children who love me. Fear not. I am the ultimate protector. From me you come and shall go. Boston is mine. I love him. He is more precious than gold. You will see great things flow from him. I restore his heart. There is nothing that has been done that cannot be un-done through my love."

I was asking the Lord about an experience that Boston, our third child, who was not quite four at the time, had had the night before. Boston had come into our bedroom to my side of the bed. He crawled in with me, which was not uncommon.

He started talking to me telling me that "God and Jesus and angels were in his bedroom."

He said that the "light had gone out the front door."

Lifted Up

When I thought that he had finally fallen asleep, he spoke again and asked me a question, "Mom, when is the builder going to be done?"

"What builder?" I asked.

Boston said that the builder was in our backyard digging. I asked Boston what the builder looked like. He said that the builder was wearing purple. Hmmm. (I later found out that purple is the color of royalty or priesthood.)

Emmelia had been born twenty-six months after Zander. Boston was born twenty-one months after Emmelia. Knox, our fourth child, was born only nineteen months after Boston. Boston was essentially a baby himself when Knox came, but by then I was totally overwhelmed by a newborn and three other young children.

Poor Boston seemed to be the recipient of all my impatience. He was not yet self-sufficient, but I made him feel like he should be when he wasn't even two years old. I have carried regret for that time in his little life. I look back at pictures of him as a two-year-old, and he looks so small and young. But at that time, I know that I expected so much of him because he was no longer the baby.

On top of that, Boston was special, in that he has very strong physical senses. He was eventually diagnosed with what the world refers to as "sensory processing disorder". What this looked like day-to-day was that he would absolutely freak out because of a tag on the inside of a shirt or because of the seam of a sock. He felt everything more strongly than other children because he was ultra-sensitive to touch. This made getting him dressed and keeping him dressed a huge challenge. I misinterpreted his complaining as misbehavior. Because he would scream and yell at me, I would then put him in time-out. He spent a lot of time in his room alone in his first few years of life.

By the time of this journal entry, Boston was really struggling emotionally. He had all kinds of problems with authority. I know now that he was such a good boy who wanted to please me, but he just was so uncomfortable because of his over-sensitivity. Additionally, as I've come to better understand the spiritual world around us—which is just as real as the physical world—I know that Boston "feels" deeply in the spirit.

One of his gifts is that of perceiving the angelic or demonic around him. I have now met several other children who have this same gift. They are often misunderstood because they will begin to act out or be naughty, but parents or teachers don't understand why. It is because they are picking up on something happening in the spiritual realm that causes them to "feel" what is going on and act in the physical realm, according to what they are feeling in the spiritual realm.

In this entry, God was reassuring me that He would restore Boston's heart. This was a tremendously important promise to me at the time. I knew that God did not want me to live with regrets for not parenting him the way that he deserved; but on my own, there was nothing I could do to make up for the loss Boston had felt in his first few years of life.

As a fulfillment of God's promise, Boston went through the Whole Heart process of inner healing himself around the age of 6. I was a part of some of his short sessions. (Whole Heart sessions happen in much shorter time frames because of the attention span of kids.) In one of his sessions, it was so beautiful to see how the Holy Spirit could take Boston back to the time when he was a baby in my arms for the very first time.

No one knew this but me, as I had never spoken of it before, but when he was born, I did not immediately bond with him like I had with my first two kids. This was because he didn't look like me. In fact, when I first held him and looked at him, I could not at all see the resemblance between him and me, or him and his two siblings. His older brother and sister had many of my features, which I guess made it easy for me to bond right away.

But for Boston, he was his own person to me. Later I was able to look at

Lifted Up

pictures of my husband as a baby and his mom and her siblings as babies. This was where Boston had gotten his dominant features.

Something else had happened not long after Boston's birth: My best friend's baby son had died tragically. As I was there for her through the mourning process during the months after his death, I faced my own grieving, which eventually became depression. Because I was struggling and was not okay emotionally, I was not able to be the best mom that I could have been. Boston seemed to be most impacted by my shortcomings during this time.

But during Whole Heart with Boston, I felt for myself a change take place between my heart and his. It was like the Holy Spirit was able to take us both back to the hospital room on the day of his birth and reclaim that moment for us of bonding. We both rebuked the lie that I could not bond with Boston because he didn't look like me. We severed the lie from our lives and placed our hurt under the cross covered by Jesus' blood, fully healed and redeemed.

From that time on, my relationship with Boston has grown and improved so much. I am able to see him for who God made him to be. Our relationship is so much closer. His teachers and others close to him could also see a difference in him take place. Where his heart had once been very closed off, he began to become tender.

Now, at age nine, Boston is a leader at school, capable of being very empathetic to others. He is caring to his classmates and helpful to his teachers. His teachers appreciate his sensitivity to the spiritual realm and have learned how to harness this gift. At Valor, he was often asked to walk through each classroom and through the halls to pray and tell any evil spirits to leave in Jesus' name. He takes this task very seriously and performs it with vigor.

4.20.14 Easter
In my prayer closet, the Lord showed me a picture of stairs, which were going up. I took Jesus' hand at the landing and he walked with me up, up, up. His hand was warm and strong. The aroma was pleasing, like the scent of peaches.

I saw a place that I knew was Valor. The building was shaped like the symbol for a dove, with a curve in the center of a V shape.

I wanted so much to see Jesus' eyes but there was some unclearness to my vision of him. He led me to the school. Valor is not just any school, but a school that raises up leaders for Christ. And they will not have to wait until adulthood to act as leaders. They will show us Christ-like faith and the faith to move mountains. We are to teach them to pray for each other, to heal each other, to heal their families, to raise the dead—all in Jesus' name.

"The beauty will radiate from them, my children. There is nothing that they will not have the power to do and to be. They are not to be like other children. Valor is not like all other schools, but what I am doing will be done elsewhere. This mission is bigger that Omaha. There is a sense of urgency that does not come from you, Rachel. It is mine, this is mine. I choose to act, and I will choose to move."

In early May 2014, Garrick and I took a trip to North Carolina. We toured a private university called High Point, in the hopes of learning about fundraising. A co-worker of mine, who was from North Carolina, had given us the reference and tried to connect us with Dr. Qubein, who had successfully raised tens of millions for the school.

We also visited a private Christian school in Raleigh. The visit to the Christian school was memorable because the superintendent of the schools met with us and shared his testimony of starting the school. They were given an unexpected gift of $20 million by a donor who had heard about what they were doing and felt God leading them to give towards the start-up. God had provided miraculously!

Both schools were beautiful and impressive in their own ways. Then, we drove on to the Moravian Falls, where we planned to attend a three-day conference before flying back home. Neither of us realized the deep impact that this conference would have on us for years to come. God had incredible and life-changing experiences in store for us at this conference!

Pray With me

Father God, Please teach me about your goodness. Help me to trust in Your goodness all the time. I recognize that my earthly father, no matter how much he tried or how much he wanted to, could never love me perfectly all the time. But you are not like this, Papa. Your love for me is good all the time. Your plans for me are good. I'm sorry, Father, for not trusting you to provide for me in all circumstances. I'm sorry for not trusting you to protect me in all circumstances. Please forgive me. I ask you to release to me a greater understanding of who you are in all your goodness. I believe the promises you have made for your children are for me too. I claim and declare those promises today over my own life:

You will fight for me; I only need to rest.   (Exodus 14:14)

You give strength when I am weary, and power when I am weak.
                                                         (Isaiah 40:29)

You take hold of my hand and you will help me. I am not to fear.
                                                         (Isaiah 41:13)

Even as the world around me shakes, your love for me is unfailing.
                                                         (Isaiah 54:10)

You go before me and you will never leave me. (Deuteronomy 31:8)

Lifted Up

CHAPTER 8: The Lies Satan tells

The conference Garrick and I attended at the Moravian Falls in North Carolina changed both of our lives in different ways. I will first share Garrick's experience through my eyes.

You might be intimidated by my sweet husband if you were to see him in a church setting prior to this. He can be the most "stoic" person you will ever meet–arms crossed, furled brow, military stance. Worship the first evening was really lovely, though by observing Garrick you would have never known it. I had my arms raised the whole night, swaying back and forth, unable to stand still. Garrick was like a statue. The conference coordinator announced that there would be a baptism offered the following morning in the Moravian Falls. To my surprise, Garrick signed us up.

The next morning, we drove over to the recreation area the Falls were located in. There was a crowd of perhaps fifty people there, all anxiously waiting to be baptized. I wrestled with the concept of being baptized in the Falls because I had received infant baptism in the Lutheran church. The words, "One baptism for the remission of sins" were ringing in my ears. I had not yet thought about laying down my Lutheran doctrine, so I almost felt guilty for considering this baptism. I eventually decided that since Garrick was my husband and the head of our household, it was okay for me to do what he did.

* Point of Clarity – In the Bible, Paul actually speaks of two different baptisms, one of repentance and one of the Holy Spirit in Acts Chapter 19:1-6,

> *While Apollos was at Corinth, Paul took the road through the interior and arrived at Ephesus. There he found some disciples [2] and asked them, "Did you receive the Holy Spirit when you believed?"*

My Whole Hearted Testimony

They answered, "No, we have not even heard that there is a Holy Spirit."

³ So Paul asked, "Then what baptism did you receive?"

"John's baptism," they replied.

⁴ Paul said, "John's baptism was a baptism of repentance. He told the people to believe in the one coming after him, that is, in Jesus." ⁵ On hearing this, they were baptized in the name of the Lord Jesus. ⁶ When Paul placed his hands on them, the Holy Spirit came on them, and they spoke in tongues and prophesied.

Acts 19:1-6

We got in line with the others. Garrick went first. He set his black flip-flops near the shore and went into the water. From my view point, nothing seemed extraordinary about what he experienced. A man helped to dunk him in the water as he blessed him. I went next. I, too, was immersed in the water. It was cold and felt invigorating. I did not perceive anything happen in the physical realm or in the spiritual realm. I walked out of the shallow stream and toweled off.

I looked around for Garrick. I saw him squatting down near the edge of the tree line a distance from other people. I saw that he was crying. He remained like that for some time.

I went to gather his flip-flops. I reached down to pick them up from where he had left them. To my shock, they were covered in gold dust. No kidding! They were completely covered. I must have gasped because someone else came over to see what I was looking at. Pretty soon, a small crowd had gathered around the flip-flops, which I was holding up for them to see.

Garrick eventually wandered over after the leader had announced that the baptisms were complete. People were heading for their cars. I was contemplating what to do with the flip-flops. I was wishing that I had brought a baggie to put them in to save them and the gold dust when

Lifted Up

Garrick grabbed them from my hands. He dropped them clumsily onto the ground and proceeded to shove his big wet feet into them. Ahhhhh! That is NOT what I would have done. I could see that his heart was very tender from what he had just experienced, so I thought twice about chastising him for not savoring the gold dust phenomena the way I was.

That night at the conference, Garrick began to worship differently. He put his hands out and up. He closed his eyes and he wept. My heart leapt for the change that was taking place in him. During the rest of the conference, Garrick would go on to have other mountain-top experiences that I would only dream of. Later he would tell me that Jesus came to him and invited him up to heaven. Garrick went with him and he said that he took my hand to take me, too. He said that once we were up in heaven, I skipped off to explore. He stayed with Jesus and was instructed by him. He said that Jesus "showed him the lay of the land".

At one point during the conference during a worship set, Garrick leaned over to me and whispered in my ear, "Holy Shit. I've got oil on my hands." I kid you not. Sure enough, I reached over and felt his hands. It appeared that oil was coming from underneath his fingernails and dripping down his fingers into the palms of both of his hands. He went to the restroom to wash his hands. When he came back with dry hands, he began to worship again and the oil began to flow a second time. I was like, give me some of that!

So that was Garrick's experience. He had zero expectation going in, and God just blew him away with love, not to mention the signs and wonders he experienced first-hand. For me, I went to the conference, very excited to see and hear Joshua Mills in person. I had seen some of his YouTube videos. His ministry was full of signs and miracles. As a naive Lutheran girl, gold dust appearing out of thin air was mind-boggling to me, though Joshua said that he experienced this regularly. Joshua learned to play the piano essentially overnight, as the Lord bestowed this gift to him so that he might lead worship. God choosing to give gifts like those seemed incredible to me at the time, and still do.

Another speaker who was going to be there was David Herzog. I had heard that it was common for precious gems to appear, or people to receive gold teeth when he spoke about Jesus. Both of these things ended up happening at this conference and I got to see them first-hand. I didn't know it when I signed us up for the conference, but God had another purpose for me in attending—beyond the signs and wonders.

A man named C. Peter Wagner had also come to speak. We met him in the hotel lobby as we checked in the first day. He was a nice enough guy. I knew nothing about him, but as he began to speak in his first session, I became totally overcome by the spirit and essentially cried and shook for each two-hour session that he led. It was crazy. Garrick wondered what the heck was going on with me. To him, this was just another old man sharing the gospel. To me, this man was helping me to make sense of who I was for the first time.

From as early as I could remember, I never felt like I fit in. I felt like I was different. My mom tells the story of how one Sunday at church, the pastor was giving a children's sermon and said the word "hell". At age two, I corrected him, telling him that he was not supposed to say that word. I had no fear. I spoke up anytime and anywhere I had something to say. I had a strong sense of right and wrong, and could easily see what others did not. I held strong convictions regarding things of the Lord, though my parents were not instilling nor reinforcing them.

As a young person, I was a leader that no one wanted to follow. I thought quickly. I was smart. I was assertive and confident. I was creative. I enjoyed solving problems. I liked coming up with plans and organizing things. I was a risk-taker. I could multitask like nobody's business. But all these traits seemed to cause only trouble for me. My assertiveness alienated people. My convictions came out as judgment against others. **Because of the many hurts and offenses, I carried in my heart, Satan was able to tell me lies about myself that I believed for far too long.**

I believed the lie that I was not worthy of love. I believed the lie that I was a mistake. I believed the lie that I was broken beyond repair. I believed the lie that no one would follow me. I believed the lie that there would never be enough (fill in the blank – money, time, resources). Satan used these lies to steal my identity. All he needed to do was place *doubt* into my head about who I was to keep me from being who God made me to be.

The things that Mr. Wagner spoke about somehow began to put order to my life and who I was created to be. For the first time, I felt like the way that I was wired was not a mistake. I also felt like I was not alone. Because I felt so different from everyone else, Satan was able to tell me the lie that I was alone in this world, and that no one would ever understand me.

I had never heard of the "New Apostolic Reformation" before. As with most supernatural things I had begun to experience since the prior October with Holy Spirit, I lacked a paradigm for what I was hearing and seeing. This allowed me to be open-minded to what I was experiencing.

As I sat there listening to Mr. Wagner, I was experiencing God in a profound way. It felt like my whole self was being shaken from the inside out. Wagner started his first talk by saying that he almost never goes anywhere unless he knows the conference coordinator personally, which was not the case for this conference. He just tells his admin to send his regrets, but this time God spoke to him and told him to go. As he spoke, I felt like he was there just for me, though undoubtedly he touched many hearts (including mine) over that long weekend. What he would share encouraged me and changed me.

I think this is a critical point to make in my testimony. Please hear me.

I did not know that what I had begun to learn about was called "charismatic" by religious circles. I just knew that I was "feeling" God in a real way that I did not know was possible. For all the Sundays I had spent in church over my whole life, I did not KNOW Holy Spirit. I did not KNOW Jesus. I knew about them but I did not KNOW them. My understanding of who God is was growing. My pastor friend, Jay, used to speak about the difference between theology (learning about God from His word), and theophany (experiencing God from Holy Spirit). I was experiencing the power of God and the love of God for the first time. I was hearing the TRUTH of who God is, and who I was made to be, having been chosen to live at THIS time and no other.

C. Peter Wagner passed away in October of 2016, but the message the Lord had given him to share lives on. Because my spirit confirmed it, I believe that Mr. Wagner truly had received revelation from the Lord about the time we are now living in, and the government that God had begun to reestablish on this earth. It's okay if you are skeptical. Take it to the Lord and ask Him for yourself. In the weeks after this conference, I read many of the books that C. Peter wrote. I also read reviews from many people seeking to discredit him. Choose for yourself.

As for me, I know what I felt that weekend and I know that what C. Peter spoke was a message for me, among others. Even as I look back now, I see a turning point that occurred in my life. I realize that no matter the lies Satan had spoken to me over my lifetime, I was no mistake. I was perfectly made for the purposes God has for me. No, I may not have ever "fit" into the mold of a sheep being led by a man. But I fit perfectly into the mold created by God just for me to be led by Jesus, my shepherd.

So, am I calling myself an "apostle"? No, I'm not, but I believe God has put a calling on my life to 'apostle'. Three different people in different settings and times have spoken this over me prompted by the Lord. Being an "apostle" has nothing to do with me. It has everything to do with God's plans and His purposes.

He could have made me to be anyone that he wanted me to be. I could have been born in 1877 as a man who would become a blacksmith. But instead, God chose for me to be born in 1977 as a female, as an engineer, wife, and mother. He chose me to be born when he did, to be "made" like He did for what He has for me...

For His kingdom which is coming on this earth. (More to come about His Kingdom in a later chapter!)

Recall from Ephesians Chapter 1:

> *"To be put into effect when the times reach their fulfill-ment—to bring unity to all things in heaven and on earth under Christ. [11] In him we were also chosen, having been predestined according to the plan of him who works out everything in conformity with the purpose of his will, [12] in order that we, who were the first to put our hope in Christ, might be for the praise of his glory."*
>
> *Ephesians 1:10-12*

I did not create myself. I did not choose this life. God chose to create me. Satan has done his best to keep me from the understanding of who I was created to be, and he has done the same in your life.

The truth is this: you were created for a purpose in the Lord.

God, your Father, loves you without end. His deepest desire is to walk with you through your life and to help you become all that He created you to be, whatever that is, and He calls it good and He calls you good!

It is this world, under Satan, that has made the terms "apostle" or "prophet" into dirty words. These are just offices, no office more important than another, but each office meant to work with another for the purpose of establishing God's Kingdom on this earth. I didn't choose to apostle but God chose this. But I do get a choice in whether I step into who God made me to be, or whether I choose to remain stuck in this world with the incomplete and inaccurate picture of my identity, according to what man says.

My Whole Hearted Testimony

I choose to seek God for my identity and my destiny, and I choose to rebuke the enemy and all the lies he would tell me about my shortcomings, my character defects, my past hurts and past sins. I want to be
only what God calls me to be. I want nothing less. I recognize that without the Lord, I am but a hollow shell. But with the Lord, I can step into
the destiny He has for me, predestined before time began—and so can
you!

Lifted Up

PERSONAL REFLECTION:

What lies has Satan been telling you? What lies are you believing about your identity and destiny? Ask the Lord to show you the lies and then rebuke them in the name of Jesus.

What are your greatest strengths? Ask the Lord to show you your strengths and write them out. It is just like Satan to use our greatest strengths against us.

What did God create you to be? Ask the Lord and see if He won't reveal to you something truly beautiful about yourself.

What did God create you to do as a part of bringing His Kingdom to this earth? Ask God to reveal to you your destiny. Reflect on past dreams that you have had. Do you see a common theme emerge?

CHAPTER 9: The Victory Is Mine

I knew that Garrick was a changed man as we flew home from North Carolina that late Sunday afternoon. He held me close. He wept openly. He spoke of doing everything together. He was so tender and willing to be vulnerable. I wish that I could say that the change was lasting, but about a month after the conference, those changes diminished. He continued to be close to God, making his relationship with Jesus a priority, but the reality of everyday life pulled him back into the world. I believe he has chosen to avoid the supernatural manifestations of God's presence such as gold dust and oil, for now. Undoubtedly the enemy has come against him and our marriage together in every way possible. But God is with Garrick and He is in our marriage and He continues to lift us up, walk with us, and wait patiently as we are transformed into His image at our own pace and in our own time.

I believe the miracles of gold dust on Garrick's shoes and the oil flowing from his finger tips are promises of things to come. And so were the memories of his tenderness towards me in that month after the conference. Of course, I wished that those things would have continued. Without ceasing for a time. If fact, I became very frustrated and impatient at Garrick for his lack of interest in the miracles and for not pursuing God like I was. I was even angry at him for not throwing caution to the wind and joining me at Valor full-time, but then God admonished me.

One night I awoke in the middle of the night. I was facing Garrick as he slept facing me. However, I didn't just see Garrick covered by blankets as he was in the physical. I saw an oak tree, complete with trunk, branches, and leaves, that appeared to be growing out of his abdomen. I heard the Holy Spirit speak to me, "Do you see what I am doing?" Yes, Lord. I see. God went on to say, "I planted the seed in him and I will grow it. Your job is to nurture the seed."

I got the message. There was nothing I was going to be able to do, or should do, to change my husband or hurry him along on his journey with the Lord. My role in his life was, and is, to love him, to respect him, to honor the work God is doing in His life. Though this experience remains fresh with me, I have to honestly say that I do not always love Garrick well. I do not always respect him the way that he deserves to be respected as the head of our family.

> "Wives, submit yourselves to your own husbands as you do to the Lord. *23* For the husband is the head of the wife as Christ is the head of the church, his body, of which he is the Savior. *24* Now as the church submits to Christ, so also wives should submit to their husbands in everything.

> *25* Husbands, love your wives, just as Christ loved the church and gave himself up for her *26* to make her holy, cleansing her by the washing with water through the word, *27* and to present her to himself as a radiant church, without stain or wrinkle or any other blemish, but holy and blameless. *28* In this same way, husbands ought to love their wives as their own bodies. He who loves his wife loves himself. *29* After all, no one ever hated their own body, but they feed and care for their body, just as Christ does the church— *30* for we are members of his body.

> *31* "For this reason a man will leave his father and mother and be united to his wife, and the two will become one flesh." *32* This is a profound mystery—but I am talking about Christ and the church. *33* However, each one of you also must love his wife as he loves himself, and the wife must respect her husband."
>
> *Ephesians 5:22-33*

I fall short and I must ask for forgiveness from Garrick and from God. I pray that I would be the wife that Garrick deserves and the wife that God made me to be. Without the Lord, I can't do it, but with God, I can do all things through Christ who strengthens me—I can even be a great wife—and all the glory will be the Lord's.

My Whole Hearted Testimony

Garrick quit his job soon after our return. This meant that I could not quit my job like I had planned to do. I've already shared with you the four-year journey since then that 've been on continuing to work at least part time while trying to lead Valor.

A change in Garrick that remained steady from the conference is the way that he worships. It doesn't matter the church we are at or what anyone else is doing or thinking. If Garrick is moved by the Spirit, he will hoot and holler, raise his hands and pump his fists. Watching him worship our Lord and Savior with all that is within him brings me such joy, and more importantly, I know that God is well-pleased!

The summer of 2014 rushed on, and though I had seen God move mightily on our trip, we still did not have a building to house Valor. The school year was set to start in August!

7.1.14 9:46am

It's July. School will start in six weeks. Will Valor be among them? We met last night and there are families that are committed to this. But where the heck are we going to meet? Ugh. Regulations, zoning, policies all seem to stand in our way. Even trying to be under the radar in our home. We just want to help the kids Father. We just want to love on them. Please, please show us where we are to be. Where are we to be, Lord?

Churches have turned away. Existing buildings aren't in the right locations. Lots of places we can't be. Where can we be?

Please help me, Lord. Please give me direction. I long to hear you in this matter.

Do you want me to give up, Father? Even as I type that, I know the answer is no. You desire my perseverance. All I can do is be an encouragement to others. It is for you to open the door for a

*"Rachel, my little lamb. I am here. I never forsake you. You are
not lost. You are not alone. Doors will open. Do not give up or
grow weary. The plan is in motion. You are only called to do your
part, not mine. You seek clarity but this world is not a clear place.
Search your heart to remove filters. I did not place them there,
you did."* He then directed me to Ephesians 6:12:

*"For our struggle is not against flesh and blood, but against the
rulers, against the authorities, against the powers of this dark
world and against the spiritual forces of evil in the heavenly
realms."*

How can I get around the powers of this world?

*"Trust in me. I can move mountains. I can create something out
of nothing. Watch. In a field, nothing stands today but tomorrow
there it is - Zion."*

Heidi suggested that we do another "Pray and Seek" to see if the Lord
would lead us to the place we were to open in the fall. On July 6th, 2014
five of us met together at a Starbucks in west-central Omaha. Heidi and
Krista departed in a car. Jeni, Kari, and I sat together in lounge chairs at
Starbucks with our Bibles open, as well as our hearts and ears to hear
what God wanted to speak to us to direct the car. We did not talk directly to the gals in the car, but we texted them as we received anything
from the Lord.

For about an hour, each of us would text any scripture, word, or picture
we felt like God was giving us. We didn't hear anything back. Kari asked
us, "When do we know if we are done?" since we had stopped receiving
any new direction. About that time, we received a text from Heidi, "On
our way back." Krista and Heidi returned to Starbucks to pick us up.
They then retraced the path they had driven and pointed out what they
saw and did as each text came in.

My Whole Hearted Testimony

This was my first pray-and-seek. (Recall that I had missed the first one that had taken place the year before, when the group was led out to Nebraska Christian.)

I was surprised to see that they had driven to the north and east. All along, I had been looking for a property in southwest Omaha where I lived. I had *thought* for the previous several years that was where God was leading us. I was wrong. When they turned onto 80th street off Maple Street, I was confused. Why were we going this way?

We pulled onto Calvary Lutheran Church property. Literally, as we pulled into the parking lot to the west of the building, I began to get physically nauseous. I looked up at the church and saw this very unique tower structure with a cross and circle at the top, and I recognized that I had seen those shapes in a picture God had given me just an hour before as we prayed. By the time we had driven all the way around the building, I was sweating, leaking tears, and ready to throw up. I asked the girls to stop the car, which they did. I jumped out and began throwing up spittle on the grass near the driveway. I sobbed and shook uncontrollably and stayed that way for quite a while. My four friends who were with me all ministered to me, as I surrendered the burden I had been carrying for so long.

Later that night I wrote this in my journal:

7.6.14
Abba, Father-I praise you and thank you. You are so good and so mighty. Today you led us to Calvary Church. Crazy things: blond girl, guy with mustache, blue horizon, black bird, electrical wires, shapes, lines that intersect. (*These were all words and pictures we were given and things and people Heidi and Krista actually saw!*)

Thank you for your mercy. You rocked me to the core. It was so good to be released from the burden. You released me. I felt your love and your joy. You are so good. There is no other God but you. You are steadfast. There is and was only you. Valor is yours. We are yours. Please work it all together in an amazing way. Lead us. We seek you and only you. Make it so Lord God on earth as it is in heaven.

Two days later, Garrick, Jeni, and I were able to meet with the Senior Pastor, Pastor Noel, and the Associate Pastor, Pastor TW. Both were very receptive to the idea of a school. To our surprise, though this church was called "Lutheran", they were spirit-led. Our story of how we were led there through prayer did not surprise them. I asked the Lord to show me how He saw this church body. He sent me to this scripture:

> "Therefore, as God's chosen people, holy and dearly loved, clothe yourselves with compassion, kindness, humility, gentleness and patience. [13] Bear with each other and forgive one another if any of you has a grievance against someone. Forgive as the Lord forgave you. [14] And over all these virtues put on love, which binds them all together in perfect unity. [15] Let the peace of Christ rule in your hearts, since as members of one body you were called to peace. And be thankful."
>
> *Colossians 3:12-15*

The wheels were set in motion. Their church board would meet soon to decide whether to present Valor's proposal to their congregation for a vote. Things were getting real!

7.12.14

Father, how are we to pay for Valor? I trust that you will supernaturally provide above and beyond what the schools needs are. Please, Lord, pour out your resources so that Garrick and I and others can do your work. Help us to end the pointless toil towards worldly gain. Please provide for all that we need.

My Whole Hearted Testimony

"Rachel. My child. I love you. You are mine. You are obedient and your ears are tuned. Do not get out in front of me, but stand directly behind me in my shadow. I will make your path straight and open each door for you. You will have all the resources you need. Do not fear. My children will come and you will reflect me love as you prepare them for battle.

Do not fear about money. It cannot be protected against evil forces of this world, but I will make a way.

Garrick is to follow me, to not look right or left. His path is in my footsteps, in Paul's footsteps. I will send him where he is to go. He will share the good news of salvation for all men who follow me. Do not lead him astray. You are to support, not command. You are to stand behind, not in front. You are and will be blessed beyond measure."

7.26.14 at 4:06am
I heard him say, *"Hear me, Rachel, you will go to Florida and be changed. You will not be the same person you are now."*

"The children will have power beyond measure. I am raising them up. They will come to you and you will equip them through me. You will face trials but I prevail. You will be given $10 million to sew into the children. I give you permission to spend money, trusting that it is my debt to pay not yours. There is no shortcut to the work of this world that must occur. Walk with me. I will carry your load. You have my supernatural favor.

Didn't I say that there would be no mistaking that this was me? When the engine roars to life, and it will roar, it is not an engine of this world. The inner workings have begun to go in motion. You feel it. I show you pieces of what is happening. Don't fret. Trust. Speak out to tell others. Seek me and I will give you the words to help them understand."

Lifted Up

Zander and I were planning to go with a group of people from the One Whole Heart Ministry to a conference in Florida called Voice of the Apostles, put on by a powerful ministry called Global Awakening, led by Randy Clark. We went in early August. While we were there, the congregation of Calvary voted to approve Valor to use their education wing as a school site.

One highlight for me that happened during the conference occurred while worshipping on one of the evenings.

At the conference, a woman fell over in front of me, laughing uncontrollably. She reached up, grabbed my hand, and pulled me down to herself. She looked right into my eyes and said, "You will have joy in all circumstances." I pulled back and she released my hand. She continued to lay in front of me, rolling around in laughter. I thought to myself, "Joy in all circumstances? Yeah, right. She doesn't know *my* life." At the time, I didn't think that it was possible to experience joy no matter what was going on around us. After all, this world is hard. The burdens of living in this sinful world are real. Of course, God would have us persevere through the struggles, which I am always prepared to do, but to have joy in the struggles? Surely that wasn't possible... or is it?

I have thought about that experience often since then. As I grow in my relationship with the Lord, I have come to believe that the statement the woman made to me was actually a promise from God. His desire for me (and for you) is that I would have joy in all circumstances. If He was making me a promise, then certainly it is possible. Though I have not yet attained joy in all circumstances, I do experience joy more often than I did. My world hasn't gotten any easier, but my perspective on living is changing.

The Lord is showing me that His desire for me and all His children is that our joy would not come from external sources—such as food, or monetary success—but internally from our Spirit-self, which is always connected to Him with Jesus as the source of His love and light.

My Whole Hearted Testimony

We've already established that joy is one of the fruits of the spirit. So, as we live out of our spirit and not our flesh, then we can experience joy. One of the sweetest blessings God has ever given to me was when I heard Him say to me, "*I have a gift to give you. Colossians 3:3.*" I turned to this unknown passage and read,

"For you died, your life is now hidden with Christ in God."

The great gift was that the Lord had told me I had died! Maybe that doesn't make sense to you but believe me, it was an answered prayer. I had been praying that I would die to myself for so long. To hear the Lord tell me that I had died brought me incredible joy. That doesn't mean that I have remained dead to self every moment since then. It is a choice to continue to die daily. There are many days I fall short and am thankful for the grace God extends me, but I press on as I claim the promise.

There are many scriptures that speak to this step of growth in the Lord. I encourage you to read these as declarations for your own life:

"Whoever does not take up their cross and follow me is not worthy of me."   *Matthew 10:38*

"For whoever wants to save their life will lose it, but whoever loses their life for me and for the gospel will save it."
                    Mark 8:35

Then he said to them all: "*Whoever wants to be my disciple must deny themselves and take up their cross daily and follow me.*
                    Luke 9:23

"Very truly I tell you, unless a kernel of wheat falls to the ground and dies, it remains only a single seed. But if it dies, it produces many seeds."   *John 12:24*

Lifted Up

"Therefore, I urge you, brothers and sisters, in view of God's mercy, to offer your bodies as a living sacrifice, holy and pleasing to God—this is your true and proper worship. "

Romans 12:1

"I face death every day—yes, just as surely as I boast about you in Christ Jesus our Lord. " *1 Corinthians 15:31*

"Therefore, if anyone is in Christ, the new creation has come: The old has gone, the new is here! " *2 Corinthians 5:17*

"I have been crucified with Christ and I no longer live, but Christ lives in me. The life I now live in the body, I live by faith in the Son of God, who loved me and gave himself for me."

Galatians 2:20

"Those who belong to Christ Jesus have crucified the flesh with its passions and desires. " *Galatians 5:24*

"For to me, to live is Christ and to die is gain. "

Philippians 1:21

So, what comes after death? Life of course! Once we have died to ourselves, then we can begin to live by the Spirit. Death in itself is not the goal but instead learning to live by the Spirit. Practically, what does this look like? I've spent the last five years trying to understand what it means to be Spirit-led. It's a term or even a label people throw around pretty loosely.

This is my personal description of what it is to live a Spirit-led life:

I can hear God's voice and follow Him. I'm able to see what God is doing in each situation and walk out His will for me in that situation.

My Whole Hearted Testimony

I am able to see others through God's eyes. I speak truth in love. All that I do is done from a place of worship of Him. My heart is fully given over to His purposes. My flesh has no place. I'm not pulled around according to the flesh of others. I have no fear of man.

I know that I have not yet "arrived" in spiritual maturity, because I cannot honestly say that every moment of my life demonstrates the principles above. But I believe that living a Spirit-led life is attainable. If having joy in all circumstances is a promise, the only way that can happen is if I am living a Spirit-led life all the time. Otherwise, joy in all circumstances would elude me.

Here is what scripture has to say about being led by the Spirit of God:

> *"As for me, this is my covenant with them," says the Lord. "My Spirit, who is on you, will not depart from you, and my words that I have put in your mouth will always be on your lips, on the lips of your children and on the lips of their descendants—from this time on and forever," says the Lord.*   *Isaiah 59:21*

> *"In the same way, the Spirit helps us in our weakness. We do not know what we ought to pray for, but the Spirit himself intercedes for us through wordless groans. 27 And he who searches our hearts knows the mind of the Spirit, because the Spirit intercedes for God's people in accordance with the will of God."*
> *Romans 8:26-27*

> *"Since we live by the Spirit, let us keep in step with the Spirit."*
> *Galatians 5:25*

> *"Whenever you are arrested and brought to trial, do not worry beforehand about what to say. Just say whatever is given you at the time, for it is not you speaking, but the Holy Spirit."*
> *Mark 13:11*

Lifted Up

"My message and my preaching were not with wise and persua-
sive words, but with a demonstration of the Spirit's power, ^{5} so
that your faith might not rest on human wisdom, but on God's
power.

^{11} For who knows a person's thoughts except their own spir-
it within them? In the same way no one knows the thoughts of
God except the Spirit of God. ^{12} What we have received is not the
spirit of the world, but the Spirit who is from God, so that we
may understand what God has freely given us.

^{13} This is what we speak, not in words taught us by human wis-
dom but in words taught by the Spirit, explaining spiritual reali-
ties with Spirit-taught words."   *1 Corinthians 2:4-5, 11-13*

"But when he, the Spirit of truth, comes, he will guide you into all
the truth. He will not speak on his own; he will speak only what
he hears, and he will tell you what is yet to come."
                                                              John 16:13

Zander was eight years old when we attended the conference in Florida.
In one of the children's sessions, he had been worshipping and was on
his face on the ground. A man named Will Hart was ministering to the
children teaching about the love of Jesus and the power of Holy Spirit.
A couple of years later, Will Hart would visit Valor and pray over our
children. He was such a blessing! The Spirit moved mightily during his
visit. Children were touched in a new and special way. Will has gone on
to lead Iris Ministries, founded by Heidi and Ronald Baker, a missional
organization headquartered in Mozambique, Africa.

Zander did not tell me right away what he had experienced that day at
the conference. A day or two later, he casually brought up how Jesus
had taken him to heaven. What?! Of course, I was excited to hear what
had happened, and I was blown away at God's goodness to invite Zander into the heavenliest. Talk about faith building!

My Whole Hearted Testimony

In writing this book, I asked Zander to retell me what he had experienced that day. I asked him if he was able to remember. He told me "Of course, mom. I remember everything that Jesus showed me. I won't ever forget!"

He said that it felt like his spirit had been pulled out of his body. He knew it was Jesus that was pulling at his spirit. He said that he saw Jesus' face. He had a short beard with hair past his ears. He brought him up to heaven. It felt like every movement was worship in heaven. Jesus brought him into a building that looked like a church. They went in together. There were three people present: one man was wearing a suit with a tie. He was carrying a flower bouquet. There was a woman in the front wearing a bonnet and a long white dress. The third man was wearing a blue suit. The shirt that he was wearing didn't match at all. The shoes he was wearing were goofy-looking. They were blue and red. He was carrying a staff. Jesus didn't tell Zander who these people were.

Zander walked to the front of the church. He knew that a wedding was being planned. God spoke to him and said, "The wedding will commence in a timely manner." (Zander did not say this, but I believe the Lord was showing Zander the Marriage (Supper) that is to come between Jesus and His bride!)

Then, Jesus took him out of the church and told him that he had something else in store for Zander. Jesus took him to a big white house in a green grassy field up on a hill. The *atmosphere* was different in this place than it had been at the church. There, he went inside the house and saw people dancing all over the house. Women and men were dancing in joy, even up and down the stairs. Then, Jesus took Zander up the stairs and he saw his Grandpa Jerry's friends from when he was younger. One of the friends was named John. Jesus said that the name John would stick forever because that was the name that was intended forever. There were two other men there who hadn't gotten their heavenly names yet.

Lifted Up

Once Zander said goodbye to these three men, Jesus brought him to a different room that was on the main floor. He showed him that the people were partying. There was wine on the table. The wine was a pleasant thing. They weren't getting drunk from it, but it was a representation of Jesus' blood. People were playing cards and having fun. There was worship music coming from a different room.

Then, Jesus brought Zander down into the lower level. He covered Zander's eyes. Zander was feeling a longing for his grandpa. Jesus then removed his hands from Zander's eyes and Zander saw his Grandpa Jerry standing before him. He looked like he was in his thirties, though he had passed away in 2013 in his late 70's. He was tall and strong looking. He was wearing a navy polo shirt that had a cross on it with diamonds around it. He had a bolo on around the collar just like he used to wear when he was alive.

Grandpa Jerry signaled to Zander to come over to him with his hand, so Zander walked up to him. Jerry then opened his arms and Zander stepped into his embrace. They hugged. The words that were spoken by Jerry after the big hug were "I love you and I always have." Then Jesus walked Zander out of the house. They started walking back into the church atmosphere. A second before they changed atmospheres, Zander heard his grandpa yell, "Come here" so Zander ran back to him and they hugged again. Jerry told him a second time, "I love you and I always have."

When they entered the church realm again, he saw two boys and one girl, and a tall, pretty, white-haired woman. Jesus said to Zander, "This is your future family." Jesus told him the names of his children. His first son was named Kyle. His second child was named Charlotte. His third and last child was named Ryan. Jesus did not tell Zander the name of his wife.

Jesus directed Zander to jump. When Zander jumped, he was back in his earthly self in the physical realm, lying on the floor of the conference hall, surrounded by other youth.

My Whole Hearted Testimony

Since that first experience with Jesus, Zander has been blessed to talk often with Jesus. He has been given many dreams and visions of heavenly things. He told me about a vision that God gave to him where he saw a 9.5 earthquake hit a place in South America called Rio Branco, Brazil. In the vision, he watched the Christ The Redeemer statue fall in Rio de Janeiro. In another night-time vision experience that went on for many nights, he spent time with King David but David was in his late teens. He had Zander stand at his right hand. Zander was told to bring in his harp. David was the only one who could play the harp.

One evening in 2015, Zander came to me wide-eyed. He said that he had just seen a cow standing in the hallway. A cow? As I probed for more information, he described to me that when he was coming out of the bathroom after brushing his teeth, he saw a calf that was standing up facing him, so that it was only standing on its back two hooves, but its eyes were at Zander's eye level. He said there was a box under the calf. I asked him if it was a platform and he said yes. The calf looked like a real animal. It was not a statue.

As I took Zander's encounter to the Lord, I believe that He confirmed a first thought that I had had about this incident. God was showing Zander a picture of an idol in his life, and perhaps in a greater way, in our family and in all of God's children. Recall that when Moses came down from the Mt. Sinai with the Ten Commandments, he was incredibly angered to see that the people had built a false God made of gold in the shape of a calf.

I have seen many profound things in the spiritual realm, things that sometimes bleed over into the physical realm that we live in.

I believe God always has a purpose in showing us things or allowing us to experience things that are beyond the natural– they are supernatural.

His heart for us is that we would seek Him to understand the purpose because He always has a purpose. In the busyness of life, I am guilty of moving on from things too soon, or even forgetting things God has shown me. As a parent, one of my most important duties in raising my children is to teach them to seek out understanding of the things of God. What precious gifts we are given by God, which carry with them responsibility.

I was Zander's math teacher for his 6th grade year. One afternoon, all of the children in his class, including Zander, were working on their math lessons. I was grading homework and monitoring the class. Everything seemed normal in the classroom to me. Zander stood up and came over to me. I thought he was going to ask me a question about his assignment, but when I looked at his face, he looked shocked. He began to whisper to me that while he was doing his math, he suddenly heard a voice speak to him and heard it clearly say, "Gabby will be your wife."

—-

To back up, over the previous summer, we were swimming at a local pool when Zander met a girl about his age. She was a cutie with long, light blond hair. They were instant friends and spent the rest of the afternoon swimming together. This was the first and only time Zander had made friends with a girl. He is a boy, through and through, and still in the stage where girls are yucky. The girl's name was Gabrielle, but she went by Gabby. It was very surprising to see Zander playing with this girl. The two were inseparable for several hours. When Gabby had to leave at the end of the afternoon, she came over and introduced herself to me and asked if she could share phone numbers with me. It was very innocent but something in my heart saw that day something my head could not have explained.

—-

Zander was completely freaked out for the remainder of the school day. Now whenever Gabby's name comes up, he gets an instant smile on his face. His siblings like to tease him about her, but he handles it really well. He has a maturity about the topic beyond his thirteen years of life. He believes what Holy Spirit spoke and he trusts God to guide his life. He has told me that he is glad because now he will have no reason to date and get distracted by girls. As a momma, that makes me happy! I don't know for certain why Zander was given the opportunity to see his grandpa after his death, or why Jesus showed him his future children, or why the Lord shared with him their names and the identity of his future wife, but I have a hunch. God is a really good God. He loves Zander deeply.

He knew how much losing his grandpa had hurt Zander, so he allowed him to see his grandpa one more time, to encourage him and to heal that hurt that was born of loss. I believe that Jesus showed Zander his future family as a promise of his life to come. I definitely am reminded to pray for her and her family often. And it will be all God's glory when these things come to fruition. The glory is His alone!

Zander had been asking a lot of questions about what would happen between now and the time Jesus comes, and what will happen after Jesus comes and reigns on this earth for his millennial reign (Revelation 20). I believe that the Lord wanted Zander (and me) to know that though things are going to get very difficult before Jesus returns during the time of the great tribulation, Zander WILL have a future family. He will be a husband and a father. I personally believe his children will be a part of the first new generation living with Jesus on this earth.

> *"Yours, LORD, is the greatness and the power*
> *and the glory and the majesty and the splendor,*
> *for everything in heaven and earth is yours.*
> *Yours, LORD, is the kingdom;*
> *you are exalted as head over all. "*
> *1 Chronicles 29:11*

Here is the deal... one-third of the Bible is prophecy. This is fact. So much of it has come to pass perfectly according to the word of God. Not one thing that is written in the Bible foretelling events has been able to be disproved. However, a great deal has been **proven accurate** with historical and archeological records. Why would God choose to make known the end from the beginning (Isaiah 46:10)? The simple answer is that He desires that His creation would know that He alone is God. The victory is His, not man's and certainly not Satan's.

158

In the same way, why would the Lord show an eight-year-old his future? Could it be that the Creator of the Universe wants this young man to know that nothing in his life is left to chance?

That God is the God over his life, and the life of every one of his children that chooses Him.

I believe Zander still has choice. He can choose to follow God's will for his life. God has shown him the fruit that will exist from following that path. Zander can choose to follow God's plans for his life day by day, moment by moment. As his mother, and a lover of God, I pray daily that Zander would choose God's path for his life!

Only time will tell if what Zander says that God showed him about his three children and wife comes to pass the way that he described. As his mom, I can choose to believe Zander and encourage him, or I can choose to disregard what he says he experienced, and in that way discourage him and his relationship with the Lord. I choose to trust Zander, but more importantly, I choose to trust God working in Zander's life.

I choose to pray for him and ask that the Lord would bring all that he showed Zander into being. And when it comes to pass, it will be all glory to God for what He spoke and what He did in Zander's life. The victory is the Lord's.

I choose to trust God and the promise He gave to me to that I will experience joy in all circumstances. I know there is nothing I can do out of my own strength to make that come to pass, except to surrender. I pray less of me and more of you, Lord. I ask Him to cause my flesh to die daily, so that I can step into the fullness of who I was created to be.

I pray that the Spirit that is in me that is connected to Him would propel me forward, teaching me to walk by Spirit and not by flesh. I choose to give glory to God because He deserves it. He has already moved in my life so abundantly as I experience more joy today than I ever did before.

I can see the fruit of His plans in Garrick's life and I praise God for that. I choose to exalt God for all the ways He has already blessed Zander and for the promises of future blessing. The glory is God's, and God's alone. There is nothing I can do to make anything come to pass, except to pray and trust God for His goodness.

STEP OF FAITH

Have I stretched your experience of God in this chapter?! It's okay if my promise of joy or Zander's experience with Jesus and his grandpa in heaven is outside your comfort zone.

I encourage you to seek the Lord for yourself. Ask Him to rebuke or confirm what I have shared. God is the same God yesterday, today, and forever. He is unchanging.

Ask Him to send you to a Bible verse that would speak truth into your life about what His victory in your life looks like.

Make no mistake about it: God has a tremendous plan for your life. Yes, Satan does his best to convince us of lies in order to steal our future— but truth always prevails. As you walk with God, and follow His path for your life, your life will begin to glorify Him in ways you can't even yet imagine! You are His treasure. You are His child, and it is all His glory to see you step into who He created you to be.

CHAPTER 10: I Call My Children Back to Me

Valor Christian Academy opened in September, 2014. Because the facility remodeling was not yet completed at Calvary Church, our first month of classes were spent at a YMCA less than a mile away. We had nineteen students total and nine families led by our administrator and teacher, Jeni, two other full-time teachers, and three other part-time teachers.

I wished that I could tell you that our first year of operation was easy but it was anything but. I did not realize how far we were from the model of education that God wanted to bring forward. We faced many significant trials, all of which He has used to cause our flesh to die and His plans to come forth. On the surface, to a casual observer, I know that what we have done has looked absolutely crazy. Let me give you some examples.

We knew that the Lord told us we were to accept any child that He called. He chose to call families to Valor who could not afford tuition. Four months into the first school year, we were not able to make payroll. I had wrongly assumed that we would pay teachers and staff a salary or hourly wage, and had signed contracts to that effect before the start of the school year. School started in September, but by March of the following Spring, all the paid staff chose to leave—except for our Spanish teacher, Mrs. Williams who was retired and did not need to rely upon the money. She comforted me by reminding me that she was serving at Valor strictly because the Lord had called her to do so.

I completely understood that Jeni and the other teachers needed to be able to *make a living*. They had bills to pay and families to feed. There was a very intense meeting of Valor's board, the staff, and others who represented the interests of the teachers. One of the attendees admonished me for lack of foresight in "counting the costs" quoting this scripture:

Lifted Up

"Suppose one of you wants to build a tower. Won't you first sit down and estimate the cost to see if you have enough money to complete it? For if you lay the foundation and are not able to finish it, everyone who sees it will ridicule you, saying, 'This person began to build and wasn't able to finish.'" Luke 14:28-30

Compounding our financial challenges was the reality that remodeling of the Church's education wing cost five times what we had budgeted. Though on the surface, the classrooms looked perfect for our purposes, the City and State requirements for school facilities required much more work than we anticipated. The bills started to roll in. I was able to pay the first few, but there came a time when there was just no more money left in the bank account.

Without tuition income, or any fundraising infrastructure in place, there was little hope. Hadn't God supernaturally led us to this location? Yes, He did, so He must have known what it would cost. Hadn't I heard many promises from Him for provision? Yes, I had. Surely that meant that the provision would be there when we needed it, right?

I was working at a consulting job to earn as much as I could. Without the consent of my husband, I was pouring funds into Valor like crazy but I was unable to keep up with the outflow. I would not recommend this approach! Thankfully my husband has forgiven me for dishonoring him by not involving him in the financial decision making. Recall, too, that we were building a lake house at this same time. Wouldn't you know it, that it was coming in well over budget as well. The verse in Luke 14:33 goes on to say,

> *"In the same way, those of you who do not give up everything you have cannot be my disciples."*

Well, I will tell you this truth. Launching Valor in the way that we did nearly cost me everything, though I was happy to give of myself because it was all I had to give. The strain on my marriage was tremendous. As a mother, my stress level was at an all-time high, which is really saying something. My temper with my kids was short, and they also felt a lot of uncertainty with the fighting that was going on at home between me and Garrick because of finances. The pressure I was under also caused my professional work to suffer, not to mention that my heart was just not in engineering anymore. God had changed my heart, and I knew it was for the better, but why did it seem like everything was falling apart just when the vision for the school was getting traction?

When all the dust settled and we had paid all that we could, we still owed $76,000 towards construction debt and another $31,000 in back payroll. We had almost no income coming in or promise of future revenue. After the paid staff left, I thought Valor would surely close, but God delivered what was not a small miracle. One of our parents and my dear friend, Kari, was a certified teacher. Though she had three little ones at home, she agreed to step in as a teacher for the remainder of the year. Another certified teacher, Kim, happened to be going through Whole Heart at that time with Heidi. Heidi asked her if she would be willing to teach at Valor through May and she also agreed. Amazingly we were able to finish out the school year.

While in the midst of this trial, I felt like I had failed. I thought that I had failed all the people who had been a part of the mission to start Valor. I thought I had failed the teachers and staff to cause them to have to abandon what felt like a sinking ship. I felt like I had failed all the families who had enrolled their children in Valor, trusting that we would be viable for at least a whole school year. I thought I had failed my own four children and husband for all the resources of every kind we had poured into Valor.

Did you catch a theme in those statements? The word "I" is used a lot. I believe God used this time in my life to teach me a very valuable lesson. I was shouldering the weight of Valor myself. I acted as if it was *my dream* to launch a school. If it would have been wildly successful at that time, (instead of the messy less than perfect launch) then wouldn't it have been for my own glory? I knew this was not my heart. I knew that for any good thing to come from Valor, it had to be His. The Lord was teaching me that this dream that He had given me was His and not mine, and because it was His, all the glory must be His – as well as the burden.

This was the lesson I learned: I am responsible for doing my part and God owns the outcome.

All that God asks of each of us is to listen to Him and follow Him. The biggest mistake I made was not listening to God *closely enough* to understand what it was He wanted to build. I assumed that Valor was to be like every other Christian school in our country. I was wrong. He wanted it to be like no other Christian school, because He was releasing a new model built on Kingdom Principles. Perhaps if we would have waited to launch another year or more, it may not have been as painful. But maybe it would have been. The best way to learn is to step in and try something, right? That is what we did. Just like riding a bicycle, you have to fall a few times before you start to get the hang of things. We fell, but God has picked us up over and over again in His goodness and mercy, and He has healed every banged up elbow and knee along the way!

Through this difficult time of not being able to pay employees, God showed us that for that season at least, our teachers and staff were to be unpaid missionaries, raising their own support—thereby relying on Him for their provision, and not on me alone or the other families. He also showed us that we were to move away from operating as an accredited school under state regulations. We reorganized to function under homeschool rules, which then allowed us to be able to accept any teacher that God called, without the state requirement that they be licensed. Both of these things allowed us to become missional in nature, which coincidentally is God's nature. He spoke to us about coming out from under the "Babylonian system" where money rules people, to move into a place where money (resources) serve us, His people.

On **May 10th, 2015**, in the midst of all the turmoil with the school launch, the Lord spoke this encouraging word to me providing clarification and hope for the future of His plans:

> *"The covenant I make with you is for this generation and all generations. I am your God and you are my people. It has always been so. I bring to you peace and hope...*
>
> *I will show you many things. It is good to seek me. It is good to want to tell others. I do not want you to get distracted from your purposes in me. I have called you to be a mother to thousands. The children will come to you, many parentless. They will be despised by this world for my sake. But I will give them shelter. I will show you how to train them up to fight for this world. You will bring hope to the hopeless, but it is not as you think.*
>
> *I have not called you to educate the minds of the children only. Your primary purpose is to purify the hearts of the children, so that they can hear my voice and follow me... My remnant will be given the power to travel the world offering healing in my name. My children will speak of salvation like never before and it will be like honey to the tongue. It will be like a soft breeze to the hot laborer.*
>
> *I place a distance between myself and the prideful. I seek the humble and the gentle. There are so many children that I desire to commune with daily. I created them for a purpose. This is no small thing. In their very core is my fingerprint... a part of me so pure and so holy that grown men will weep and cry out in their presence as my spirit is manifested.*
>
> *Every child is precious to me, and **every** child has a purpose. I have not called (the school) into being to meet the needs of **every** child. And I will not call every child to (the school). You must seek me to discern those I am calling. I will not be manipulated by a mother's cry or a grandmother's plea. Just as the woman that*

touched my son's cloak and who was healed of the blood disorder, I will have mercy for each family and each child and care for them in my way.

A child carries the sins of many generations on his back, so to a child carries the blessings of many generations in his heart. Do not question my ways, for you do not know my ways. It is not for you to understand for you cannot. My ways are not your ways for My Kingdom has not yet come. But we stand at this time, divided only by a thin veil, where one can see and nearly touch heaven. The time is fast approaching when my son shall ride on a cloud of glory to this earth, when every person shall see his beauty and gaze upon his countenance, the perfect sacrifice, the perfect peace, the perfect representation of my love for my people. Before this time, death and destruction must come, the wheat must be separated from the tares. I carefully comb the earth looking for those who call out to me, who long to be held by my embrace, who see that I've created them for something more. I will rescue my people and I will reign victorious with them for eternity.

Though the times to come are perilous, I make a way. I have blessed you by boiling out the sores that festered just under your skin. I make you new. If you are not made new, you cannot taste of the goodness I have for you, or touch of the softness, or hear the lovely notes that flutter in the air to delight your ears. In time, I will make all things new, but for now, only a portion experience these gifts I have to offer. I know that it has felt like pain and anguish to be overwhelmed by the responsibility of the vision I've given to you. I come to you to proclaim that there is an easier way, and you know this to be true. I give you rest when you allow me to. Every heart beat is a chance to rest in me.

You must die to live. You must surrender to be free. You must love to be loved. You must forgive to be forgiven. You must teach to be taught. You must cry to be comforted. You must nurture to be nurtured. You must rest to have the energy to carry out your purposes in me. Time is running short. You must spend more time with me and less time in things of this world. My plans for you are secure. Walk with me that I may reveal all these things to you. You ask what your identity is in me. You are my bride. You are my first love. You carry my heart with you. You are no longer to hide it away but instead put it on display for all to see.

You are a warrior, but you also are a servant. You are a mother, but you also are a child. I've created you to be tenderhearted, so be. I've given you discernment, so be wise in the words that you speak, seeking me for the full measure of understanding. You are tender, and it is not weakness but strength. Jesus gave his life for you that you may stand by his side, holding his hand."

We are living at a time when God is moving mightily to **call His children back to Himself**. He is reaching the lost and the lukewarm alike. I was one of those who was living a life on the outskirts of faith. I said that I believed in Jesus as my Savior but there was nothing in my life that reflected this statement.

Simply going to church one hour a week does *not a disciple make*. There was nothing **about** my life that looked any different than a non-believer's life—until I encountered the Holy Spirit, causing God's Word to come alive. And then, as I surrendered my own will to God, Jesus was able to take up residence in my heart as He healed it and made it whole.

You can see from my own tale of failures that following God and even hearing His voice does not mean that we are guaranteed success, at least by the definition for success that this world relies upon. Though the story of the birthing of Valor is full of the flaws of my own human nature, it is also full of His grace and mercy towards me as His child.

Lifted Up

If you have given your life to the Lord and are willing to follow Him, then you can be assured that He has a "life's work" to reveal to you tied to His Kingdom. Maybe you are fortunate enough to already know what that is. If so, bless God! If not, I encourage you to "count the costs" and then dive headfirst into all that He has for you, beloved one!

He knew when I would fail, yet He loved me anyway. He knew that I would rebel, but He never stopped loving me or calling out to me. It is the same with you, dear child of the one true God.

My Whole Hearted Testimony

<u>Questions to ponder and take before the Lord:</u>

What is the calling God has placed on your life?

Will you accept the commissioning God has for you?

Is the Lord calling you to enter into the Covenant with Him? If so, what is the step of faith He would have you make to draw close to Him, seeking His will for your life?

<u>CHAPTER 11: Who You Are In Me</u>

In this chapter, I want to share with you a some of the key practical differences between the educational model God has given to us in Valor and the existing educational system that is prevalent in our country. You may find this insightful for your children or grandchildren, or for yourself in better understanding how you learn, grow and are filled up to pour out. As parents or grandparents, we have the opportunity to teach our children at any time, according to how God made them in His image. These lessons the Lord has been teaching us through Valor in a school setting are just as applicable at home interacting as families, or even together with other families in community with each other.

In the Fall of 2015, the school began its second year of operation. The number of families involved grew, as did the number of students. Some-how God had made a way when all had seemed lost. Who would think that a school could operate without charging tuition on a volunteer ba-sis alone? Though no one was being paid a salary, we had more than thirty volunteers active in our second year!

The Lord continued to do a work in our hearts, helping us to lay down any preconceived ideas of what "school" should look like so that He could show us **HIS** model for educating **HIS** children. The debt was still present, but little by little, those we owed were being paid and extend-ing us grace.

On **August 11th, 2015,** during worship time, the Lord placed this mes-sage on my heart:

> God's (model for) education is a gift to teachers. Valor is a gift for any teacher He calls. It will be like setting them free to do what God has called them to do.

The calling of a teacher is just as critical and important as the calling of an apostle, prophet, evangelist or pastor.

My Whole Hearted Testimony

Recall from Ephesians 4:11-12:

> *"So Christ himself gave the apostles, the prophets, the evangelists, the pastors and teachers,* [12] *to equip his people for works of service, so that the body of Christ may be built up ."*

Each office was instituted by God. My heart breaks for the teachers in our country and other countries, who no longer have the freedom to teach according to their calling. On this journey with Valor I've had the opportunity to meet many passionate and excellent teachers. A common regret I hear from them is their disappointment in not having the time or the freedom to connect with their students in a meaningful way during the school day.

I know from my own journey what a critical role my own teachers played in pulling me up from the pit of despair. Mrs. Banks and Mr. Wilmot changed the course of my life because of the truth they spoke into me at critical junctures in my life. Because they were *in relationship* with me, I was able to receive from them when they chose to pour out their wisdom and their heart to me.

Today, the majority of our public school classrooms are filled with so many students, making it quite impossible for a teacher to connect with the heart of each student. Yet, without this heart connection, how does a child learn that their life has value? How does a teacher know how to reach each student if they don't have the capacity or time to really get to know each child? God could have made all of us like little cookies all cut using the same cookie cutter, but He didn't. Instead, He made every one of us completely unique, like a snowflake, not one the same. How would it then make sense to expect to teach each child the same way, or for each child to learn the same way? It doesn't.

At Valor, God has shown us the importance of recognizing the learning style of each student. There are three primary learning styles: Visual, Auditory and Tactile (also called Kinesthetic). A visual learner prefers the use of images to access and understand new information. An auditory

Lifted Up

learner best understands new concepts by listening and speaking. They use repetition as a study technique and benefit from the use of mnemonic devices. Lastly, the tactile learner best understands information through hands-on learning and figuring things out by hand. The reason it is so important to recognize each child's learning preference is that it unlocks a mystery into the best way (the most efficient and fun) to reach them.

If your child is struggling in a large classroom where the teacher spends most of the time lecturing, it could be because their primary learning style is not auditory. If they are a tactile learner, they benefit from an environment where exploration and experimentation is valued. If they are a visual learner, they would likely benefit from an environment rich with pictures and examples of the concepts being taught. There are simple assessments available online to guide a parent in determining a child's learning style.

Personally, this facet of how we are shaped has been very valuable. My daughter, Emmelia is left-handed. She is over-the-moon creative, seriously. She can make anything out of cardboard and duct tape. She loves to draw and paint and cut and paste. She is musically gifted with a sweet voice. She enjoys gymnastics and dance. She has a natural ability for problem-solving. You can see from these characteristics that there is nothing *wrong* with her mind or body. However, when it came to basic concepts in math, she struggled dearly.

She dreaded math time each day and would look for ways to get out of it like complaining of a stomach ache magically at the same time each day. When we could get her to sit down to work on math, tears would just start flowing. I thought it was just me as her math teacher so I asked for help from others and they had the same result.

It wasn't until after Emme had taken the learning style assessment that the Lord highlighted to me that the curriculum she was using for math was not the right fit. Emme's assessment showed that she was primarily a tactile learner with a secondary visual aspect. I had given her Saxon math, assuming that it would work for her like it had for Zander who excelled in this format.

Another Valor mom recommended that we try out Math-U-See which is built especially for tactile and visual learners. Students use small blocks of different colors based on one's, two's, five's and ten's. Students use these blocks to be able to touch and see the concepts that are being presented. It is this physical interaction that cements the learning in the brain. Since we have switched to this curriculum, she loves math and is doing well. Most importantly, she doesn't feel like there is something inherently *wrong* with her because she doesn't learn like everyone else.

Another key attribute God has highlighted to us has been recognizing each child's love language. Gary Chapman writes in an online Focus on the Family article, "My conclusion after many years of marriage counseling is that there are five emotional love languages — five ways that people speak and understand emotional love." This wisdom can and should be applied to children as well. The five love languages as defined by Chapman are: words of affirmation, quality time, receiving gifts, acts of service and physical touch. A quick assessment will show the primary love language of a child and their secondary love languages too.

Let me give you a practical example. As a mother of 4 children, I know from experience that it does not work when I try to relate to and love all my kids in the same way. What I've found is that my oldest son, Zander, needs hugs every day, but my daughter Emmelia shrugs off my hugs like they are no big deal. However, if I don't spend time with her over a few days, she will tell me how sad she feels because her "love tank" is empty. In order to fill it, I've found the best way is for us to have some one on one time together shopping. This is usually so that she can pick out gifts for other people, because her primary love language is gifts and her secondary is quality time.

My son, Boston, gets his love tank filled when I sit next to him and we watch a movie together. His primary love language is quality time and his secondary is physical touch. My youngest son, Knox, needs me to cuddle with him every day as often as possible. When he starts to misbehave, I know the best way to soften his heart is to pick him up, hold him close and maybe give him a tummy zerbert until he starts to giggle. I have logged hundreds, maybe thousands of hours tickling that child's back and tummy. He can't get enough!

Recognizing each child's love language is critical because how can we expect them to learn and grow when their love tank is empty? But when their individual needs for being loved are met, it is amazing to see how the fertile soil will produce lasting fruit. If you don't know them already, I encourage you to do a quick google search of love languages to complete an assessment for yourself, your children, or anyone that you would like to love better.

My prayer for teachers is that as God builds His Kingdom of education on this earth, they would again be freed from teaching according to the ways of this world, but would instead be allowed to seek God and speak truth into every student, according to their God-given identity and destiny in God's Kingdom.

At Valor, we pray for and over the children regularly. As hurts arise, we pray with them for forgiveness and repentance as a part of leveraging the One Whole Heart model. It's not complicated. We invite Holy Spirit in to guide and comfort us and the student who we are ministering to. We then ask the child what emotions they are feeling. (We use pictures to help younger students identify their emotions.) The child will share any background about what is bothering them so that they learn that they do have a voice and that what they think and feel matters. But we don't get bogged down in the opinions or the facts of the situation. What is most important is who they need to forgive and for what, what they need to repent for to receive forgiveness, and that the Lord's presence comes into the situation to bring His peace.

I recently came across material that simply demonstrated the roots of our current educational system in the United States and perhaps across the globe. It contrasted the Hebrew system as given by God to His people through Abraham who was a Hebrew (pre-Israelite) with the later man-made Greek system that now guides modern education. I literally cried as I read through this slide and my heart leapt. I realized that what God had been showing us at Valor and leading us towards was not new! In fact, the guiding principles He had been revealing to us were right there describing the Hebrew system in black and white!

"The Greek system emphasizes knowledge, with the students learning what the teacher knows. This is based on cognitive input; the act or process of putting knowledge in. The Hebrew system is a scriptural model of education and the goal is for the student to BECOME what the teacher IS. Knowledge is acquired as a by-product, while the goal is to shape the character of the student."

In the Hebrew model, "the belief is that students are powerful (by divine design) and their hearts and minds need molding." This is contrasted with the Greek model which supposes that "students' minds are empty and need filling."

Think about how different a teacher's approach would be depending upon the paradigm they hold towards their students. I was not an educator by profession. I did not go to a Teacher's college and so I did not have a paradigm towards teaching. In fact, I never really thought of myself as a teacher, even in the first few years of Valor's operation. I believe that it was because of this naïve open-mindness that I was able to receive what the Lord was showing me related to His desires for the model of education. And then, in His goodness, He brought me a confirmation through this material of the truth of what He desires towards the mountain of education.

In the Hebrew model of education, how important is the teacher in the process? The teacher is critical since the goal is for the student to become what the teacher is! Aren't we to become like Jesus? Yes, of course. That is the goal of every believer to be a disciple of Jesus. Contrast that to the American education system which relies so heavily on curriculum (where philosophers are the source of all information) for control of the educational process. Didn't I joke as a child that "Those that can, do. Those that can't, teach." In the Hebrew model, this is far from the truth. The value of an adult walking in the Spirit and not in the flesh teaching our children to do the same could not be greater. As disciples of the Truth, our deepest held belief must be that God, through His Word, is the source of all true knowledge.

August 17th, 2015
Is there anything you want to speak into me tonight, Lord?

"Rachel, my daughter. I call to you and you listen. This delights me. You are precious to me in every way. I am a proud papa, daddy. I give you good gifts because I love you and desire to increase your joy. Your happiness brings me joy. I am proud of the progress you've made in laying down your own cross to carry mine. You are doing well. You know that I have more for you and I'm waiting patiently to bestow upon you my favor in other areas of your life.

In Valor this year, I am well pleased with the planning and diligence you and your team have undertaken. The pieces of the puzzle are coming together gloriously. I appreciate the place of honor you are creating for me. You will feel me in great and small ways in every area of the building, in every area of your heart, and in every place in each child.

I will wash the debt away. You will feel as though you have more room to breathe, and you are now in a state of beginning to breathe me in more freely, more fully.

In your marriage, I am there - you both have invited me in and I am happy to hold both your hands and walk with you.

I have remade you, daughter. The death has occurred and you never have to go back to your old self. Let her die and bury her, and then turn your eyes to the heavens to gaze upon my glory and the glory of my Son.

He is coming back to take his bride. There is much to be done. Bless you, child. Rest and open your heart to me tonight to fill you like never before."

God's heart for each of us is that we would know Him more, and that we would be able to see ourselves through His eyes. Isn't this what relationship is all about? He created you for relationship with Him. He delights in encountering you and giving you opportunities to encounter Him.

God is so much greater than what most of us give Him credit for. If you believe this, then perhaps you can believe that who He created you to be is much greater than you could have ever imagined before. The Lord wants to help you to let go of self-doubt and place your full faith and trust in Him for what He can accomplish in and through you.

During Jesus' life on this earth, He did some incredible things. He performed so many miracles that the Bible says there aren't enough pages to contain them all. Jesus demonstrated the heart of God to love unconditionally, to encourage, to heal, and even to raise the dead.

> *"Very truly I tell you, whoever believes in me will do the works I have been doing, and they will do even greater things than these, because I am going to the Father. [13] And I will do whatever you ask in my name, so that the Father may be glorified in the Son. [14] You may ask me for anything in my name, and I will do it."*
> *John 14:12-14*

In the last few years, I have witnessed many healing miracles through prayer spoken in Jesus' name. It is never with our own authority that we could pray, because we have no power apart from Jesus who lives in us. But in Jesus' name and the authority that comes through Him, I believe there is no limit to what God can and will do to love His children. I have seen legs grow out. I have seen knee and hip pain go away. I have witnessed the evidence of a box and two tubes being removed from a

Lifted Up

man's brain when someone prayed for him to be healed of hydrocepha-
lus.

"Heal the sick, raise the dead, cleanse those who have leprosy,
drive out demons. Freely you have received; freely give. "
Matthew 10:8

The greatest miracle I have experienced personally happened on October 18th, 2015. We were at home and I had just come upstairs. I was
standing at my dresser, putting away clothes. Zander and Boston were
wrestling around in the living room downstairs like they usually do. All
of a sudden, I heard Garrick yell my name. I knew something significant
had happened because of the tone of his voice. I turned to walk down
the stairs and I had supernatural peace in my heart because I knew that
whatever had happened, it would be alright. This is not normally my re-
action! Something was just different this time. It was like a gift of faith
came over me.

I met Garrick on the stairs holding Boston. He told me that Boston's
wrist was broken. I asked Garrick if I could pray for Boston. I knew that
Garrick was genuinely frightened about what he had just witnessed. (I
later found out that Boston's hand had hit Zander's calf and caused it to
bend backwards until it snapped.) Boston's hand dangled awkwardly
with bones no longer attached to support it.

Garrick handed Boston over to my arms while he ran back down the
stairs, frantically preparing to leave for the ER. I started praying and
took the wrist in my hand. It did feel floppy. Boston had fear in his eyes
and was crying loudly. I prayed a simple prayer, "Jesus, I pray healing of
Boston's wrist in your name." I then touched Boston's wrist with my
fingers and it was like the strength returned. I told Boston to move it
and he was able to lift up his hand and swivel his wrist up and down
normally. Surprise crossed his face as he stopped crying.

I came down the stairs, still carrying Boston. Garrick had fear in his voice
and would not look at me. He just kept saying that we needed to get
Boston to the hospital. I told Garrick that God just healed Boston. Gar-

rick spoke to me, "Not now, Rachel. He is really hurt."

I told Garrick to see for himself. Boston showed his dad that he could move his hand normally. Garrick said to me, "But I heard it break."

I could see that he was trying to process what had just happened in his mind. He sat down with Boston on the couch and just began to rock with him.

In the meantime, Zander was freaking out screaming in tears that he had broken Boston's wrist. He was sitting on the floor next to his wall, bumping his own head up against the wall. He felt so bad for what had happened. I have never seen Zander so distraught.

He told me he felt it break. But I told him that God healed Boston's wrist and that he was going to be totally okay. It took Zander a minute to calm down. I held him. I told him that I knew that it was just an accident and that he was forgiven. I encouraged him to go see for himself that Boston was okay.

When the break happened, I just had total peace. It was nothing I could have created on my own. The peace was a gift from God. I heard God tell me a little later that, "Perfect love casts out all fear." God, in that moment, gave me His perfect love. He gave me the faith to believe that Boston would be healed, and he was. I praised God for what He had done. It occurred to me that a wrist fracture could have really impacted his life. He is such a good little athlete. He is a natural wrestler, and loves to play football and basketball with Zander.

To have to wear a cast for weeks would have been so hard on him, physically and emotionally. And, there could have been long-lasting effects with a severe break like that that could have altered his future, perhaps keeping him from what God had for him. God chose to bring healing through my prayer.

Lifted Up

Praise God that He has not left us powerless. Through Jesus Christ living in us, all we have to do is call on His name to not only be saved, but to be healed. We serve the only God with that kind of power. The question that I cannot answer is: why does God not heal every hurt or every disease when someone prays?

A sweet little boy named Joey, just as awesome as Boston, broke his arm right in front of me, falling out of a large trash hopper while playing near a fireworks tent on the 4th of July, 2017. I ran to him and placed my hand over the obviously protruding broken bones of his small right arm. I felt the bones move back into place under my grip. I prayed with fervor and I believed that he would be healed, just like Boston was, though I did not feel the same supernatural peace I had felt the moment Boston's wrist broke.

The ambulance soon arrived and medical help was ready to attend to him. I had to literally *will myself* to release his arm so that they could see the broken arm and begin to stabilize it for travel to the hospital. I knew that when I took my hand off his broken bones that they had not been repaired. I cried out to the Lord, begging him to heal this beautiful child, to save him from the pain that would come–but immediate healing did not occur, though I knew it was possible. Everyone Jesus prayed for was healed, and He instructed us to heal the sick. If he commanded it, then surely it is possible.

> *"Immediately the boy's father exclaimed, "I do believe; help me overcome my unbelief!"*　　　　　　　　　　*Mark 9:24*

God is the God of miracles. He is unchanging. What He has done before, He can do again. God is capable of using you to work miracles on this earth through the power of Holy Spirit in Jesus' name alone. It is no different with young ones. In fact, we find that younger children have a much easier time trusting in their own prayers to the Lord because of the simple faith they hold. At Valor, God has made it clear to us the importance of prayer for His Body. Children, just as adults, are to know how to pray. There is not one perfect recipe for praying for healing but the most important element is the faith to believe God will answer. To aid in learning and practicing, here is the model we use at Valor when we pray for physical healing:

Model for Prayer of Physical Healing

First introduce yourself and ask the other person's name.

Ask the person if there is anything that is hurting or anything they need prayer for.

Ask the person if it is okay to lay hands on them (such as touching their hand or shoulder).

Invite the Holy Spirit to come.

Pray a simple prayer in Jesus' name. It is not the length of the prayer that counts!
"Jesus, please heal (_____) of (_____) or
"I command healing of (_____) of (_____) in Jesus' name" or
"All pain in (_____) go in Jesus' name".

Ask the person to test out the area that was hurting.

Ask the person if they see a change in that body part. If so, praise God! If not, still praise God for loving the person.

Ask the person if you can pray one more time for them if they are not fully healed.

If there was some change but not total healing, then praise God for what He has done and ask "for more healing to come" or "full and complete healing in Jesus' name".

Re-interview the person to determine if more healing has come. Praise God for what He is doing in their life and thank Him.

Lifted Up

We aren't to seek the supernatural for the novelty of it, but I believe it is okay to want to experience the fullness of God. Moses wasn't afraid to ask God to see His glory! (Exodus 33)

It's okay to ask God for His best for you. He will choose what that looks like and feels like for each of us. It is also not just about me or you—it is about each person He wants to touch. If you are a willing vessel, God will use you to bring healing of heart or body into another one of His children. They will be blessed when this happens and so will you!

> [29] *Now, Lord, consider their threats and enable your servants to speak your word with great boldness.* [30] *Stretch out your hand to heal and perform signs and wonders through the name of your holy servant Jesus."* [31] *After they prayed, the place where they were meeting was shaken. And they were all filled with the Holy Spirit and spoke the word of God boldly...*

> [33] *With great power the apostles continued to testify to the resurrection of the Lord Jesus. And God's grace was so powerfully at work in them all* [34] *that there were no needy persons among them. For from time to time those who owned land or houses sold them, brought the money from the sales* [35] *and put it at the apostles' feet, and it was distributed to anyone who had need.*

> *Acts 4:29-31, 33-35*

Personal Reflection:

**If you have never done this before, consider offering to pray for some-
one else (in their presence) for healing of some kind.** Try using the
model I shared in this chapter, or just ask the Lord to give you the words
as you step out in faith.

**Do you know someone who could really use prayer right now and may
be open to it? Or would it be easier for you to go up to a stranger to
offer to pray for them?** Choose to step out in faith and pray for someone today!

There are so many great resources available for learning more about
healing prayer and miracles for today. Here are some of my favorites:

John G. Lake Ministries called the Divine Healing Technician Training
    by Curry Blake   (Youtube online video series or www.jglm.org)

Jeff Randle Pillar Power School at www.unveiledlife.org

Randy Clark's ministry of healing through Global Awakening
    (www.globalawakening.com)

Documentary video series by Darren Wilson – Furious Love, Father
    of Lights, Holy Ghost, Holy Ghost Reborn, Finger of God 1 and 2

Todd White Youtube videos on healing

CHAPTER 12: The Great Harvest That is Coming

Prayer is a sound that goes forth in the physical realm that reaches the throne room of God, which then has the power to change physical circumstances. Here is an example from Daniel when He sought the Lord in prayer for understanding: the angel, Gabriel was dispatched immediately but Satan came against him to prevent him from reaching Daniel until Michael, another arch-angel of God, joined in to free Gabriel.

> *Then he continued, "Do not be afraid, Daniel. Since the first day that you set your mind to gain understanding and to humble yourself before your God, your words were heard, and I have come in response to them.*
>
> *[13] But the prince of the Persian kingdom resisted me twenty-one days. Then Michael, one of the chief princes, came to help me, because I was detained there with the king of Persia.*
>
> *[14] Now I have come to explain to you what will happen to your people in the future, for the vision concerns a time yet to come."*
> Daniel 10:12-14

There is a preparation underway in the spiritual realm for what is about to happen in this world of the physical realm. I have seen this so clearly in the changes that have occurred in my own heart, in a short span of six years. I know that I am not alone in receiving revelation from God of His plans and His heart for this generation that will see His Son return. As He shares his heart, we are to pray His heart back to Him. This co-laboring with His creation is His way of bringing about the fulfillment of His Kingdom, delayed by Satan in the Garden but not prevented.

God is calling to us to understand the times we are living in so that we can be active participants in those plans! Isn't that exciting? He doesn't want us to just sit on the sidelines and watch. He wants us on the field and in our stance, ready for the play to be called. We are to be "prayed up" and ready to execute. God spoke to Ezekiel, Daniel, and John instructing them to seal up the scroll. Based on what the Lord has spoken to me and shown me, the time of the scroll being sealed has ended. We are living in the generation of the fulfillment of all of God's plans. Holy Spirit distinctly spoke these words to me during a supernatural experience in May of 2015 and I believe them:

"The scroll is being opened."

I believe that this means that God will give us understanding of His plans in a way no other generation has had. The purpose? Because it is now time for the fulfillment of those plans, and those plans include the realm of education which is really just the equipping of God's people according to His grand design.

Sept. 3, 2015 at 2:12am
I woke up with the words "*It is not yet time for the fullness*".

Abba, Father, what would you like to say?

"My creation is a grand design. From Day 1 to the last day, every day is preordained for a purpose. While we have reached the fullness of times in the last days I have for my creation, we have not reached the time of my fullness. The great harvest is upon you and the preparations for that are good in me. I desire for you to go where I send you. I've told you that I will send you out and I will call you home."

I heard – *"Rachel, I have something for you"* and felt like I should come into the closet. All my kids are sleeping in my room tonight and my husband seems irritated with the light from the iPad as I type.

What do you have for me, Lord and giver of all life? I heard, *"Answers."*

"You are my servant and I am well pleased. You are my daughter

and I am a proud papa. You are becoming my bride and my heart swells with the love I have for you."

"I desire to define the work of Valor. I have told you that Valor, the work I have for Valor, is not for all people. This is not something I choose to do to call to all. Valor is a work I am doing to raise up the people who will usher in the great harvest. You are forerunners of things to come. You are my gift to the world. I am calling to my children who have been chosen before time began. This is not an elitist work, for it is nothing you earned. I preordained this work for this time and for this generation. I am calling these people, adults, and children—my people—to a deeper understanding of who I am and who you are in me.

When I say that it is not yet time for the fullness, I mean to express that it is not yet the time for my full expression to be known in my children—but that is coming, and the preparation for that is required, so that your hearts are ready to receive all that I have to offer.

Your hearts cannot possibly contain all that I am, all that I have for you. I must do a work in you first to cause your hearts to swell. The truth is that you are mine and I am yours. The truth is that I send the call out to all my children who have been called to this time. I wait to hear the response. Will my call be heeded? With every response from every nation, I desire to send another out to meet them where they are, to show them the way into the deeper place.

You ask in your heart why is it that I need you when I can do all things? This is true. I need no person, yet this is your earth and beginning with my son Adam, I gave you (my creation) dominion over it. This is your planet and I choose to walk with you. I've always desired to co-labor. Nothing brings me more joy than walking with each of my children through this life with them.

The recognition that when you experience sorrow, I am there holding you. That when you experience joy, I am there. In every moment, I am there.

As you rest in me, I show you more of my heart for you. Once you've experienced this place in me, you can then share it with another. Experience by experience, you begin to reflect more of who I am, less of your fleshly nature. This is how the battle is won.

It is MY desire that you travel from place to place, releasing my kingdom. I have placed upon you the mantle of Motherhood and I have placed upon Garrick the mantle of Fatherhood. Together, the love that you share that is from me will change nations. This is all to come.

I open doors for you to walk through. I know your heart, daughter, and that you want only what is from me. It is so good that you have learned the life lessons the last three years about striving from your own power. What I have always had for you and for Valor is so much greater than you could ever contain on your own. Now you are beginning to see that which is greater than any one or two people.

The vision for my mountain of education is this: *a contrite people who have received healing of their very heart and have been taught to hear my voice and to see that which I am doing. Whole families will be called to partake, as well as individual children. I will call to them of my own doing but I will also use people to make the call known.*

This Order is global and it will take time for the connections to be made. There is nothing you need to do to make anything happen. Remember, it has already happened! Now you just step into what's already been created in the spiritual.

Lifted Up

$10 million is a good starting number! But I have so much more than this for my people. I will give you the map and the sequence of events. I will give you the timeline. I will give you the budget. I will call the people. Just rest in me, daughter.

I am taking back the education of my children from the hands of the enemy. I will bring light into dark places in a glorious manner. My light that is in my children will shine brighter than the sun! I've already placed the strategy in your heart. Now I will help you release it. I've made you many promises and my word is true. I withhold no good thing. The work that I've begun in you I will see through to completion.

Paul talks about the times reaching their fulfillment in a letter to the Ephesians. At that time, all things will come into unity in both heaven and earth under Jesus. He says:

"With all wisdom and understanding, [9] he made known to us the mystery of his will according to his good pleasure, which he purposed in Christ, [10] to be put into effect when the times reach their fulfillment—to bring unity to all things in heaven and on earth under Christ." Ephesians 1:8b-10

There is a work God is doing in me and in you to bring us back into the unity of the body He always intended, and yet was predestined to occur in this generation we have been chosen to live. Each of us has a role to play in the work that is ahead to prepare for Christ's return. My heart cries out to the Lord daily for His plans and His purposes to come to fruition in and through my life. There is nothing I can do to *make it* happen, except to surrender to Him.

On **December 9, 2015 at 3:03 am**, I was deeply asleep, dreaming of being asleep in this very large house that was grand and exquisite. It was better than any mansion I've ever seen on television. (For me, dreaming of dreaming is significant. Each time this has happened, I know that the dream holds exceptional significance for me.)

My Whole Hearted Testimony

I was in bed, asleep in the master bedroom with my husband, when I was awoken to knocking at the door. It went on for a while. Eventually I nudged my husband awake so that he could see who it was. I was a little anxious, like you would be if it had really happened. I didn't know who it was as I watched my husband leave the bedroom and walk down the hallway, down the big staircase, then start towards the door, which was quite a distance since the house was so big. He either said it or I was thinking he knew who it was as he got to the door. Just then, I was actually woken up from my dream by one of our kids.

So I got up out of bed *for real,* still thinking of the dream and wondering who was going to be at the door in the dream. I felt like I should go downstairs to get a drink of water. I went downstairs and heard the word "**centurion**."

I had the sense that a large soldier was standing in the corner of the dining room facing me. His presence was so real I felt like I should have been able to see him physically with my eyes, but I could only see him in the spirit with the eyes of my heart.

> I kept looking at the spot where I thought the centurion was. I asked the Lord, "Why is he here?"
>
> The Lord answered, "**The battle lines have been drawn.**"
>
> Then I asked, "What battle?"
>
> He answered, "**For souls, to take them to hell or to heaven.**"
>
> Then I asked, "What does the centurion want with me?"
>
> Then I heard, "**To give you plans and orders.**"
>
> Then I felt like the centurion moved to the living room and was about eight feet from me. I asked the Lord, "How do I get the orders?"

Lifted Up

I heard, "**Put out your hand and he will place them in your hand.**"

So I did and felt like he laid a rolled up piece of parchment in my outstretched hand. I asked, "How will I take them?"

I felt like he said, "**Move your hand to your heart to take them into yourself.**"

So I did. Then I felt like the centurion turned to leave out the back of the house. He mounted a horse and departed.

Later, in prayer, I felt confirmation that it was Jesus at the door in the dream. He is knocking as the time is at hand. He wants everyone of us to answer His call, and He wants to give us wisdom and understanding for what lies ahead.

"Here I am! I stand at the door and knock. If anyone hears my voice and opens the door, I will come in and eat with that person, and they with me." Revelation 3:20

Then on **December 13, 2015,** in the early evening, I heard this word from the Lord:

"Quiet yourself before me. Get rid of all distractions. I am the gentle breeze. I am a soft fabric against your skin. I am subtle. Do not lose sight of the end game, eternity with me. Stand strong, even as the winds of evil blow mighty and powerful. I will be your protection. I will be your strong tower... The schemes of the enemy are great, but not one hair on the head of one of My children will be harmed, for those that rest in the shelter of the Most High.

The centurion wears my armor into every battle. He walks in sandals of peace. His head is covered with the helmet of salvation. His chest is covered in my righteousness. His shield of faith caus-

es every arrow of the enemy to fall. His sword is mighty, cutting even to the bone with the power to create and destroy with my word. I desire every one of my children to dress as the centurion. You will face battles and you must put on the whole armor. When in it fully, your protection is complete, and victory is assured. Prepare for battle. The time has come. Do not go out without it on anymore. Teach each child to wear theirs.

Fear not that which is coming upon the earth. Everything made by man will shake. Everything built on the foundation of My Son, the cornerstone, will stand firm. I am doing a work in My children. I am pouring My love out, beyond measure. No ear has heard the glorious riches in store for My children who love me. Remember that this is temporal, temporary, but I am eternal. There is nothing that you will face that I have not already triumphed over.

Arise children of the one true God! Waive your banners! Blow your trumpets! Begin your march in step as I lead you around Jericho! For it will be I, only Me that brings ultimate victory over death. Watch as the wall falls and evil is destroyed once and for all.

Then, there shall I stand in victory, as the old passes away and the new comes forth. My bride ready for her groom!"

After this powerful word from the Lord, I sought out scriptural confirmations of the things I had heard Him say to me. This is always a good practice. When the Lord speaks to you or me personally, what He shares will always line up with His Word. If it does not, then we have to be willing to let it go assuming we did not hear correctly, and ask Him to clarify our understanding. You can be sure that He desires only that we receive TRUTH and He will lead us into all truth so that we are not deceived.

Lifted Up

Finally, be strong in the Lord and in his mighty power. [11] *Put on the full armor of God, so that you can take your stand against the devil's schemes.* [12] *For our struggle is not against flesh and blood, but against the rulers, against the authorities, against the powers of this dark world and against the spiritual forces of evil in the heavenly realms.*

[13] *Therefore put on the full armor of God, so that when the day of evil comes, you may be able to stand your ground, and after you have done everything, to stand.* [14] *Stand firm then, with the belt of truth buckled around your waist, with the breastplate of right-eousness in place,* [15] *and with your feet fitted with the readiness that comes from the gospel of peace.*

[16] *In addition to all this, take up the shield of faith, with which you can extinguish all the flaming arrows of the evil one.* [17] *Take the helmet of salvation and the sword of the Spirit, which is the word of God.*

[18] *And pray in the Spirit on all occasions with all kinds of prayers and requests. With this in mind, be alert and always keep on praying for all the Lord's people.*

Ephesians 6:10-18

My Whole Hearted Testimony

Now when Joshua was near Jericho, he looked up and saw a man standing in front of him with a drawn sword in his hand. Joshua went up to him and asked, "Are you for us or for our enemies?"

[14] "Neither," he replied, "but as commander of the army of the LORD I have now come." Then Joshua fell facedown to the ground in reverence, and asked him, "What message does my Lord have for his servant?"

Joshua 5:13-14

Then the LORD said to Joshua, "See, I have delivered Jericho into your hands, along with its king and its fighting men. [3] March around the city once with all the armed men. Do this for six days. [4] Have seven priests carry trumpets of rams' horns in front of the ark. On the seventh day, march around the city seven times, with the priests blowing the trumpets. [5] When you hear them sound a long blast on the trumpets, have the whole army give a loud shout; then the wall of the city will collapse and the army will go up, everyone straight in."

Joshua 6:2-5

In late December 2015, I was attending a conference in Kansas City called One Thing put on by the International House of Prayer, or IHOP. In the midst of the conference, I stole away to spend some time in The Word.

The Lord had had me in the Book of Daniel for some time. Mike Bickel was also teaching from Daniel at the conference. The Lord first sent me to Daniel Chapter 2. This is a quite well-known chapter. King Nebuchadnezzar had a dream about a statue made of different materials from head to toe. Daniel sought the Lord and was able to interpret the dream. Each portion of the statue related to different kingdoms that would reign in the future.

Lifted Up

What God highlighted to me in this study session caused the scripture and the promise it gave to come to life for me.

12.29.15

Daniel 2: The Interpretation - relating to the end times:

While you were watching, a rock was cut out, but not by human hands. It struck the statue on its feet of iron and clay and smashed them. [35] Then the iron, the clay, the bronze, the silver and the gold were all broken to pieces and became like chaff on a threshing floor in the summer. The wind swept them away without leaving a trace. But the rock that struck the statue became a huge mountain and filled the whole earth.

"In the time of those kings, the God of heaven will set up a king-dom that will never be destroyed, nor will it be left to another people. It will crush all those kingdoms and bring them to an end, but it will itself endure forever. [45] This is the meaning of the vision of the rock cut out of a mountain, but not by human hands—a rock that broke the iron, the bronze, the clay, the silver and the gold to pieces.

"The great God has shown the king what will take place in the future. The dream is true and its interpretation is trustworthy."
Daniel 2:34-35, 44-45 NIV

Help me to understand this, Lord. I feel like this relates to the knowing of the kingdom you are establishing on this earth now—the way you are revealing your mountain of education now so that it is already established when your Son returns.

My Whole Hearted Testimony

What I heard:

This new kingdom that is being established now will cut down every kingdom of this world.

In Daniel 2, the words used are these: "In the time of those kings". It doesn't say **AFTER** those kings and kingdoms are gone, it says **IN** the time. I believe the Lord has shown me without a shadow of a doubt that we are living **IN THAT TIME**. If I truly believe that, then wouldn't God have me do what He caused Daniel to do? Shouldn't we, as believers, seek God for the promise He gave in Daniel 2:44:*"In the time of those kings, the God of heaven will set up a kingdom that will never be destroyed, nor will it be left to another people. It will crush all those kingdoms and bring them to an end, but it will itself endure forever."*

This seems exceptionally clear to me. If we are living in the time of those kings, then we can expect that **God IS SETTING UP a kingdom, His kingdom**, and it will cause all the other kingdoms that are not of Him to fall. This scripture also says very clearly that this same Kingdom under God that is being established will endure forever.

Here is the revelation that I received on this day, which God has caused to become etched in my heart:

God is establishing His kingdom on this earth right now and He has asked me (and He is asking you) to be a part of it.

Again, He could do it all by Himself, but He chooses to co-labor with us. He has shown me that my calling at this time is to help establish His model for the education of His children. God isn't going to wait until Jesus comes, then clean the slate and start over.

Right now, God is working through His people to begin establishing His kingdom, so that when Jesus comes to live and reign on this earth, the "infrastructure", if you will, is in place.

I believe that there are tiny seeds all over this earth today of His Kingdom. God has begun giving the revelation for the many facets of His Kingdom to people who will listen and follow Him. He is pouring out His spirit in great measure on His people to do the work of His Kingdom. Recall that in Daniel 2, he speaks of *"a rock [that] was cut out, but not by human hands. It struck the statue on its feet of iron and clay and smashed them."* As I've sought the Lord for understanding, I believe what this is saying is that Jesus is that rock, for we know that He is the cornerstone.

But now in Christ Jesus you who once were far away have been brought near by the blood of Christ.

[14] For he himself is our peace, who has made the two groups one and has destroyed the barrier, the dividing wall of hostility, [15] by setting aside in his flesh the law with its commands and regulations. His purpose was to create in himself one new humanity out of the two, thus making peace, [16] and in one body to reconcile both of them to God through the cross, by which he put to death their hostility. [17] He came and preached peace to you who were far away and peace to those who were near. [18] For through him we both have access to the Father by one Spirit.

[19] Consequently, you are no longer foreigners and strangers, but fellow citizens with God's people and also members of his household, [20] built on the foundation of the apostles and prophets, with Christ Jesus himself as the chief cornerstone. [21] In him the whole building is joined together and rises to become a holy temple in the Lord. [22] And in him you too are being built together to become a dwelling in which God lives by his Spirit.

Ephesians 2:13-22

My Whole Hearted Testimony

The Lord showed me a picture of His hands coming down, reaching into a mountain and grabbing a huge boulder from the mountain side. Then it was like all of His children were packed around that boulder, like someone would shape a ball of dough. Then God threw the boulder at the feet of the great statue that Nebuchadnezzar had seen, causing it to fall.

What I believe God was showing me was that it is Christ Jesus in us (as we were packed all around Him) in unity that will cause all the kingdoms of Satan to fall. And then,

> *"the rock that struck the statue became a huge mountain and filled the whole earth."*

This is the Kingdom of God with Jesus as the head, living on earth and reigning with the children of God. The intention then, of God revealing the plans for His Kingdom now to His people, is so that the models and framework will be in place at least on a small scale to begin teaching the children of God His ways in the coming reign of Jesus on this earth. This is what I have come to believe, based on the things God has shown me and spoken to me:

We are to seek the Lord for His plans and trust that He will release them at just the right time in just the right way. I do not claim to have full understanding of all the plans for His Kingdom coming to this earth, but I do believe that the Lord has given me and others working with Valor a framework to build from for the education of His children. Day by day, moment by moment, as we seek Him, He continues to grow our understanding. These things don't have to be taught formally in a school setting and are just as applicable within a family environment. Though each of us, like Gideon, are "the least of these", God is doing a mighty work and all the glory is His.

Lifted Up

The model for Kingdom Education that God has given us:

Worship – The Lord desires to teach His children to live out every area of their lives as worship to Him, beyond just singing and dance or even art, though these are all key ways to worship. He wants His children to understand that their whole lives are to be worship to Him. As they grow into adulthood, their paradigm for living will be so significantly different than anything this earth has known since the time of Adam and Eve.

Prayer – The Lord wants to teach His children how to pray from His own heart seeing and releasing His will on this earth. It is His desire that each of His children would have confidence in the authority that He has placed in them, through their inheritance as a son or daughter through Jesus, to pray for others to be saved and healed.

Experiencing God – The truth is that God created every one of His children to hear His voice. Jesus left Holy Spirit to dwell within us so that we would always be connected to the Father. God's heart is that His children would feel His presence and be able to hear His voice in all circumstances.

Releasing the Kingdom of God – When a child knows who they are in Christ, they can release His Kingdom to others. Children are taught to live from a place of wholeheartedness, walking in continuous forgiveness of others and repentance of any sins. It is out of this place of wholeness in Him, that each child can be who He made them to be, prepared to walk out their destiny in His Kingdom.

Attaining Godly Wisdom – Obtaining the knowledge, wisdom, and skill to fulfill the call of each life according to God's purposes and His ways. The Lord God, as creator of all things, desires to teach His children about His creation from His perspective, not from the world's distorted view.

My Whole Hearted Testimony

As Christians have prayed for two thousand years: "Thy Kingdom come. Thy will be done." Valor is an answer to that prayer. It is not a building or a location as I mistakenly focused on and strove towards for such a long time. It is not to be found at Nebraska Christian College, or Faith Presbyterian, or Calvary Lutheran Church. Valor is not a school in a building. Valor is a people.

Valor is a piece of God's Kingdom being built on earth as the Lord releases His model for Kingdom Education. It is a place in God's own heart where all who come experience the love of God and the power of Holy Spirit. It is communities of disciples (children, parents, grandparents, and missionaries) being raised up and set into their destiny, connected one to another as one body, under Jesus.

> *"There is one body and one Spirit, just as you were called to one hope when you were called; [5] one Lord, one faith, one baptism; [6] one God and Father of all, who is over all and through all and in all. "*   *Ephesians 4:4-6*

God's heart is to redeem this generation for Himself. He desires that each child would know His great love for them through His Son Jesus, that they would recognize the power of Holy Spirit that dwells within them, and that they would confidently release all that He placed inside of them before the foundation of time.

I was driving with my friend, Heidi, and our two sons to another conference hosted in 2015 by Global Awakening to be held in Tennessee. While we were driving, we were worshipping. As we went through St. Louis, I found myself in the middle of an open vision. I was the one driving but somehow God kept us from getting in an accident. Heidi reached over to steer the car. I didn't have the wherewithal to pull the car over, so we did get off course and became lost for a bit!

Lifted Up

In this open vision, I saw a map of the United States as if projected in front of me. I saw a golden ring over the city of Omaha (and Council Bluffs which is just across the river), where we live today. In the middle of the golden ring, the letters 'H U B' appeared. I then saw arrows flying from other parts of the country into the ring. In my spirit, I knew that these arrows were people being sent from other cities to be equipped in Omaha. They would then be sent back out to release the Kingdom of God throughout the world.

Over a two-week period following the open vision, I continued to receive prophetic revelations from dreams, visions, and the word of the Lord coming to me. The Lord laid out for me a ten-year plan from 2016 to 2026, broken into three periods of time. The first period, called "Foundational", was for the laying and setting up of the foundation of Valor. I believe this season is nearing its end as structures are refined and processes are established with Jesus as the head.

The second period of time is called "Expansion". I believe this is the period where we will see the greatest growth in the model of Valor being shared all over the country, and the world. The Lord has clearly spoken that the model for Valor is meant to be replicable, not duplicated. In other words, what structure works for one community is not meant to be exactly the same in another community.

God is not a God of chaos, so we can trust that He will show us His structures. However, if we hold onto man-made structures, we are prevented from shifting paradigms. We are learning to follow the lead of the spirit in trying different approaches to serve children and families in education.

We worship together, we pray together, we eat together, and we learn together. This is the definition of community, and not surprisingly, this is the underlying foundation of Kingdom Education. What the Lord instituted in the beginning, He is again renewing in His people.

"They devoted themselves to the apostles' teaching and to fellowship, to the breaking of bread and to prayer. [43] Everyone was filled with awe at the many wonders and signs performed by the apostles. [44] All the believers were together and had everything in common. [45] They sold property and possessions to give to anyone who had need.

[46] Every day they continued to meet together in the temple courts. They broke bread in their homes and ate together with glad and sincere hearts, [47] praising God and enjoying the favor of all the people. And the Lord added to their number daily those who were being saved. "

Acts 2:42-47

Kingdom Education is not confined to a one-size-fits-all approach. I believe the Lord has encouraged us to try lots of different formats so that we could see more clearly that setting children into their destiny has little to do with the schedule, but more to do with the position of our hearts to Him and one another. A healthy fully-functioning community of believers will be made up of adults and children: who have received inner healing so that there is nothing that separates them from the love of God, who hear God's voice, and walk in the Spirit.

The 3rd and final period of time the Lord showed me is called "Maturity", where the Kingdom model for education (and all the mountains of His Kingdom) will be known and understood by those in the body of Christ. This is also the time where I believe the Bride of Christ will begin to come into maturity, so transformed that when the broken world looks at us, they will no longer see you or me, but they will see the true love of God through Jesus in us.

I believe the Lord showed me that the purpose of the schools and the communities that will be raised up is to prepare for and participate in the *Great Harvest* that is ahead of us. The start may not be far away!

I have set my heart to praying for the fulfillment of that promise!

Lifted Up

Pray with me

Our Father who art in heaven. Hallowed be thy name. Thy Kingdom come. Thy will be done, on earth as it is in heaven. Father, you promise that as I seek you, I will find you. Your Word promises that I have been created for a divine purpose in you before the foundations of this world.

Lord God, I come before you as a child of God, your child. I was made in your image. I was made for such a time as this to know you, and to know who you created me to be. I trust you to finish the good work you began in me. I trust you to lead me into all the goodness you have for me. I ask you to release to my understanding the revelation you have for me as a part of your Kingdom being built on earth. Give me your wisdom and understanding. Give me your wise counsel as I endeavor to follow you and to share the gospel, the good news of Jesus, alive and active in our lives today. He was and is to come again soon!

I pray, Lord, that you would strengthen me in my resolve to follow you and to let your Spirit lead me into all truth. I love you. I give you my heart, all of it. I boldly declare Your Kingdom Come in my life and in the lives of those I love! May you be lifted up in all the glory that is yours, even as you lift me up out of this kingdom into Your Kingdom which is come!

For more on the work God is doing through Valor today, or to learn more about Kingdom resources available to you and your family, please check out: www.ValorCommunity.com

My Whole Hearted Testimony

CONCLUSION

"Worship God, for the testimony of Jesus is the spirit of prophecy."
Revelation 19:10 KJV

My prayer is that this book about my own journey and the birthing of Valor is a testimony of what Jesus has done in one life, and what He **can do** in another. I was dead but now I live through Him that lives in me. You can see that apart from God, my life was nothing special. I was just a broken vessel being held together by Elmer's glue at best. Through the heart healing I received, by learning to hear God's voice, and by choosing to follow Him, my life has been redeemed. I do not claim that I "have arrived" at any destination of perfection, but I have grown and will continue to press on with the Lord as long as there is the breath of life in my lungs.

I have attempted to shine the light on how encountering Holy Spirit in late 2013 has not only changed my perspective on my life, but changed my life itself. Jesus ascended into the heavens but He did not leave us powerless!

I continue to dream of flying often. Just last week, I dreamed that the Lord had immersed me in water; and when I came out, I floated up and couldn't keep my feet on the ground. I don't yet fully understand the significance of flying in my life, but I believe there is one. Truly the Lord has **lifted me up** in more ways than one!

I'd like to share one last supernatural experience with you before I close that ties in with being *lifted up*. This is the most special to me of any experiences (theophany) the Lord has given me because I got to spend time with Jesus Himself *physically*.

> It was in the late hours of the night when all of a sudden, I found myself standing in the middle of our kitchen, facing the patio door. I then felt and saw one hand come and touch my left shoulder and begin lightly rubbing it. Then a second hand ap-

peared on my right shoulder and began rubbing my shoulder and neck. Then I knew that it was Jesus; as he looked over my left shoulder and smiled, He was standing behind me, holding me tenderly but with strength.

Then it was like we blasted up into the air through the ceiling, into the sky and eventually into the outer atmosphere. I could feel the strong breeze blowing past my face with such power. I tried to open my eyes, but they could not open because of the wind blowing past my face. I had thought that it was strange that I was not getting cold. Then it was like we stopped, and I knew that I was still in Jesus' arms.

I was able to open my eyes and look around. I could see our planet, (a sphere of glistening blue and white like I've seen in photos from space before, but so much more sharp in brilliance); and then I looked around and could see the universe including other planets and stars of light. This was all happened in what felt like a split-second. Then we were blasting back down so fast towards what I thought was the earth. For some reason, going in this direction, I was able to keep my eyes open. We zipped through a layer of clouds and then it was like we arrived at a place that Jesus had chosen for us. (Later, I would recognize that it was a heavenly place, not our earth as it is today.)

There was water like you would expect in a shallow natural pool. I was sitting in the water on my bottom and it was only waist-deep. At first Jesus was right next to me and I could see small sharks circling playfully around us. I was a little nervous at first, but then Jesus took my hand in his and held it out to one of the sharks to show me that they could not hurt me. It just nuzzled the ends of my fingers and did not bite them. He said, "*Do not be afraid.*" (of course!)

It felt like we were all childlike but that we were also adults. In other words, age was not relevant to the experience in this heavenly place. It felt playful but it was also a place for instruction. Jesus then was sitting over to the right about ten feet from me with other children next to Him. He was watching all of us and enjoying us while interacting with us. Strangely, even though we were in water, I was not experiencing the sensation of being wet.

As I reflected on this beautiful and very special experience, I see how amazing it was that the Lord answered the prayer I had prayed before I fell asleep that night. This was my prayer to Him that night:

> "I'm just a mess, Lord. I am sorry for being so stubborn. I am sorry for wanting my own way. I am sorry for ever going ahead of you. Please forgive me. I repent of every sin. The truth is that I am lost without you. I am nothing without you. I need you in every part of my life. I find that today I have come to the end of myself, again. Have your way, Lord. Your will be done.
>
> **I ask you to allow me to see you with my eyes.**
>
> I ask you to allow me to see your angels. I ask you to allow me to see what the Father is doing.
>
> **I ask you to give me eyes to see what you see, from a heavenly perspective and not an earthly one.**"

Do you see how God chose to answer my heartfelt prayer? He let me see Him and even feel Him. Then He took me up to the heavenlies to see a different perspective of the earth—the one that He sees. It is interesting that it felt like we went back down to earth, but it was unlike anything on this earth today. It was a place of incredible beauty and peace. Could it be that this is how He sees the earth, in its redeemed form?

I am not the same person I was before the end of 2013, because I began to have an actual relationship with Jesus and became a friend of God, by surrendering my own will and seeking Him through prayer and worship.

Lifted Up

The process of death to self is difficult, but it is well-worth it. I learned the difference between living by the flesh and walking by the Spirit. I've encountered the promise of God to have joy in all circumstances and hold tight to that promise.

I learned that God had a purpose and a plan for my life, even before I was born. He taught me that as I find my identity in Him alone, fear of man can die and I can become who He made me to be. His love for me comes not from what I do for Him or for anyone else, but simply for who I am in Him.

I learned that God does not see me as the sum of my past mistakes, but instead He sees me through the lens of the finished work Jesus did on the cross. That finished work means that my heart and your heart can be fully healed, so that we can hear God and see what He is doing. It means that we can live so that the enemy has no place in us and has no power over us.

The Lord Himself has taught me about the gifts of the Spirit that He still gives out freely today. I pray that my life would testify that the gifts are still in existence today. He wants us to use them according to His purposes, for His glory, as he chooses to co-labor with us on this earth. Just as it was in the days just after Jesus ascended to His heavenly throne, so shall it be in the days we are living just before He comes to take His rightful earthly throne.

> *Peter replied, "Repent and be baptized, every one of you, in the name of Jesus Christ for the forgiveness of your sins. And you will receive the gift of the Holy Spirit.* [39] *The promise is for you and your children and for all who are far off—for all whom the Lord our God will call."*

⁴⁰ With many other words he warned them; and he pleaded with them, "Save yourselves from this corrupt generation." ⁴¹ Those who accepted his message were baptized, and about three thousand were added to their number that day.

Acts 2:38-41

The Lord has spoken to me over and over again that He is calling His children back to Himself. His heart is that every single person alive today would turn to Him, and call on the name of Jesus to be saved.

Each one of us has a part to play in this "Thy Kingdom Coming" mission. The harvest is plentiful but the laborers are few. Won't you surrender your life today to join in the mission?

My testimony is not complete and neither is yours. As long as there is breath in our lungs, we have an opportunity to serve the mighty God of the universe who created us for relationship with Him.

"Worship God, for the testimony of Jesus is the spirit of prophecy."
Revelation 19:10 KJV

CALL TO ACTION -

Do you feel the call of God on your life? Has He called you to Kingdom Education or to another facet of His Kingdom that is coming to this earth?

Make no mistake. You have been called to co-labor with Him for the advancement of His Kingdom which is coming. The question is whether you will respond to that call with a resounding "YES" from your spirit, or whether you will turn away and hide your face from the only one who truly knows you—who you were created to be and who you can step into beginning even today.

Ask the Lord to show you His heart for you. Ask Him to make it clear what dream He has placed in your heart. Then, make a commitment to walk with Him moment by moment to seek out the fulfillment of that dream. You don't have to have it all figured out to begin. You just have to take the first step.

What is the first step God is calling you to make today? Allow Him to show you, and then take that first step hand-in-hand with the one who loves you with an everlasting love.

AUTHOR'S BIO

Rachel Rebecca (Marienau) Baxter was baptized, confirmed, and married in a Lutheran Church, Missouri Synod in a small town in northwest Iowa. She fell away from the faith of her childhood in her late teens, but came back to the Lord at age 25 in 2002. She married, Garrick Baxter, in 2003 and they have 4 children.

Rachel received her Bachelor of Industrial Engineering degree from the University of Nebraska, Lincoln. She earned her Master's of Business from Portland State University. She worked as an engineer in manufacturing for 10 years, and then transitioned to business efficiency consulting helping companies improve processes.

Rachel became spirit-filled in late 2013 and received deep inner healing in 2014 through a ministry called One Whole Heart. www.onewholeheartministry.com

It was at this time that she began to hear the voice of the Lord. The Lord began to give her dreams and visions of the things that will come to pass in the years ahead prior to Jesus' return. He began instructing her to write His words to the nations and the Body of Christ. In the fall of 2015, she began to share these words from God's heart as a warning to repent, and for the Bride of Christ to prepare for the Bridegroom's return. These words can be found at www.scrollandfigleaf.com.

The Lord called Rachel to lead an effort to start a spirit-filled school called Valor Christian Academy which began in 2014 in Omaha, Nebraska. Valor's mission is to equip communities of believers being raised up for the great harvest that is to come - to prepare both children and families for the destiny that He has for them in the exciting years ahead as His Kingdom comes. www.valorcommunity.com

www.ingramcontent.com/pod-product-compliance
Lightning Source LLC
Chambersburg PA
CBHW031621040426
42452CB00007B/612